Mere Ecclesiology

Mere Ecclesiology

Finding Your Place in the Church's Mission

J. Gregory Crofford

Foreword by Jo Anne Lyon

WIPF & STOCK · Eugene, Oregon

MERE ECCLESIOLOGY
Finding Your Place in the Church's Mission

Copyright © 2016 J. Gregory Crofford. All rights reserved. Except for brief quotations in critical publications or reviews, no part of this book may be reproduced in any manner without prior written permission from the publisher. Write: Permissions, Wipf and Stock Publishers, 199 W. 8th Ave., Suite 3, Eugene, OR 97401.

Wipf & Stock
An Imprint of Wipf and Stock Publishers
199 W. 8th Ave., Suite 3
Eugene, OR 97401

www.wipfandstock.com

PAPERBACK ISBN: 978-1-5326-0421-8
HARDCOVER ISBN: 978-1-5326-0423-2
EBOOK ISBN: 978-1-5326-0422-5

Manufactured in the U.S.A.   OCTOBER 27, 2016

All Scripture quotations, except otherwise noted, are taken from The Holy Bible, New International Version®, NIV® Copyright ©1973, 1978, 1984, 2011 by Biblica, Inc.™ Used by permission. All rights reserved worldwide.

Other Bible versions used:

Scripture quotations are from the Holy Bible: International Standard Version®. Copyright © 1996-forever by The ISV Foundation. ALL RIGHTS RESERVED INTERNATIONALLY. Used by permission.

Scripture quotations are from the Holy Bible, New Living Translation, copyright ©1996, 2004, 2007, 2013, 2015 by Tyndale House Foundation. Used by permission of Tyndale House Publishers, Inc., Carol Stream, Illinois 60188. All rights reserved.

Scripture quotations are from the Holy Bible, English Standard Version, copyright © 2001 by Crossway Bibles, a publishing ministry of Good News Publishers. Used by permission. All rights reserved.

To my brothers, David and Todd Crofford,
colleagues in ordained ministry and
companions on the journey:

Your passion for Christ and love for the church inspire me.

Contents

Foreword | ix
Acknowledgments | xi
Introduction | xiii

1   The Church: God's Holy People | 3
2   Following Jesus, Together | 9
3   Beyond Self: Gathered to Worship | 15
4   Preach It! | 21
5   Come to the Table | 27
6   Baptism: Joining God's People | 36
7   Prayer and Fasting | 41
8   Christian Education: Digging Deeper, Building Higher | 45
9   Independence or Interdependence? The Power of Small Groups | 51
10 God's Not-So-Secret Plan to Save Creation | 57
11 Healing and Deliverance | 62
12 Discover Your Calling | 72
13 Impact Your Community | 79
14 Ecology for Christ Followers | 84
15 Love without Limits: Sharing Christ Cross-Culturally | 92

Conclusion | 98
Bibliography | 101

Foreword

THE COMPELLING STATEMENT OF Christopher J. H. Wright—"The church does not have a mission in the world. God's mission has a church in the world"—is one that is sometimes haunting. On the surface we can say "Amen," but when it comes to tools in which to live this out we are lacking.

The church particularly in the West has become an observer sport. People many times attend church on Sunday morning and an NFL game in the afternoon all with the same attitude. But if the church is God's mission in the world, it will not survive as a spectator sport.

Greg has powerfully captured the church—"God's mission in the world"—in these brief pages. Ecclesiology is generally a subject written and discussed in academic theological circles and rarely reaches the person in the pew. But this is one for the pew and will be valued as well.

The metaphor of "breathing in" and "breathing out" will deepen the understanding of ecclesiology in practice. For far too long these concepts have been in competition, contrasted, and even argued as to which is the most important. Greg has relied on Scripture, church history, contemporary issues, global understanding, and personal experiences to add texture to this holistic approach to ecclesiology.

I believe one of the reasons for overall declining membership in the church, particularly in the West, is that there is no challenge. Membership in church many times is seen no more than belonging to Sam's Club. People simply belong to Sam's Club because of

Foreword

personal gain or that of getting a discount on items. There has been discussion in some circles that churches need to offer something similar to gain membership. This is polar opposite to "God's Mission in the world" and simply has put the church on a consumer basis.

Mere Ecclesiology is a tool that can reverse these ideas and practices. "Breathing in" is the depth of people becoming more like Jesus personally and becoming who we were made to be. "Breathing out" is participating in God's mission in the world as God intends it to be.

I look forward to seeing the transformation that can come to churches as they take these principles seriously and we will begin to realize the *church* as God's mission in the world as God intended it to be.

Jo Anne Lyon, Ambassador
General Superintendent Emerita
The Wesleyan Church

Acknowledgments

ANY ENDEAVOR OF THIS magnitude is never a solitary endeavor. Amy Crofford, my wife, was an excellent sounding board for ideas. Fili Chambo, my former supervisor, also took a keen interest in the book as it evolved.

Though he is long departed, my childhood pastor, Rev. Morris Wilson, shaped my youthful imagination. More than anyone else, his preaching and leadership set the tone that made Trinity Church my second family and—most importantly—the place where God came close. If my mind is now convinced of the importance of the community of faith, then no doubt it is because my heart was long ago persuaded under Rev. Wilson's godly and winsome ministry.

Several individuals took time from their busy schedules to read early drafts of the book, making helpful suggestions. Ben Jones, Gift Mtukwa, Gabriel Benjiman, Dave Crofford, and Brad Crofford—thank you. Doug Hardy also suggested a shorter, less ambitious outline. The result is better for it. On the concept of interdependence, Dany Gomis sparked my thinking.

Finally, thank you to Mike Adams for his anointed preaching at camp, triggering a life-changing and surprising word to me from the Lord. Perhaps God will see fit to speak a similar word to the church today.

Introduction

CHRISTIANITY SEEMS HOPELESSLY FRAGMENTED. Thousands of denominations dot the landscape and more are born each year. Little can Martin Luther have known in 1521 when he attached his ninety-five theses to the door of the cathedral in Wittenberg what forces that one act would release. In the face of such a dizzying array of churches, is it possible—like C. S. Lewis attempted with his *Mere Christianity*—to identify a "mere ecclesiology" (doctrine of the church), a core motif that unites the people of God despite our incredible diversity? Some have described this twofold movement as being "gathered to worship and scattered to serve." In *Mere Ecclesiology: Finding Your Place in the Church's Mission*, a similar idea is what I call "spiritual respiration," the body of Christ (1 Cor 12:12–31) breathing in and breathing out. No matter the denominational affiliation of a congregation (or none), a basic life function for any church is this inward and outward movement. The notion of spiritual respiration helps us visualize our life together as the people of God, God first transforming us ("breathing in") then the Holy Spirit sending us out in loving service to transform our world ("breathing out").

A few years ago, I revisited a campground in the Catskill Mountains of New York, the same camp I frequented during summers as a boy. That Sunday morning, the preacher did what I had seen preachers do many times when I was younger. He invited people to come forward to pray. While kneeling, I sensed God speaking to me clearly: *"Greg, prayer is just spiritual respiration. So why are you holding your breath?"*

INTRODUCTION

God's gentle advice to me on that Sunday regarding prayer is also good counsel for the church. The image of "respiration" reminds us as God's people to live in the rhythm of God's Holy Spirit. It helps us understand both our corporate encounter with God ("breathing in") and our service together in the world ("breathing out"). Both are essential. Just for fun, take a minute and try only breathing in. It doesn't take long before your lungs feel like they're going to explode! Now try the opposite. Breathe out, pushing air from your lungs through your mouth and nose. Soon, your lungs are empty; you have no air left to exhale. You simply must take another breath or else faint.

Shortly after his resurrection, Jesus appeared to his disciples. He breathed on them and said, "Receive the Holy Spirit" (John 20:22). It may seem a bit strange at first that Jesus would do this. What did he mean? Could it be that this little group of men—a seed of the much larger church that would be born at Pentecost—needed to learn a lesson about how the Holy Spirit works through his church? Breathing indeed is a metaphor for how the church is to function in the rhythm of God's Spirit, gathering together for worship and mutual encouragement (inhaling), then scattering for transformational service in the world (exhaling). This model of the church—to borrow the words of Clark Pinnock—is a "Spirit ecclesiology."[1]

Usually when we think about breathing, we think of it individually. However, it can be a group exercise. When we learned that we would have a baby, my wife, Amy, and I signed up for childbirth classes. For several weeks we met with other expectant couples. A veteran obstetrics nurse gave us information about what we could expect when the "big day" came. Yet a large part of our time together was spent learning how to breathe, to take deep breaths then to fully exhale. As husbands and wives, we breathed in together, then together, breathed out. *In-out, in-out*—the rhythm of respiration relaxed and calmed us. It later gave me something to do when labor struck!

---

1. Pinnock, *Flame of Love*, 114.

Introduction

Some churches are excellent at breathing in. They preach a clear gospel message that God wants to forgive us and change us. Such churches realize that the most important decision that any of us will make is to follow Jesus; they constantly call people of all ages to repent of their sins, to be saved, helping them afterward to grow in their faith. Often, they host Bible studies and prayer meetings. They believe in *personal* transformation. Yet the same churches may have trouble breathing out. When you look at how they spend their corporate calories, few are expended on impacting their community through service. They are ingrown, not yet understanding that God wants to use them as salt and light, to bring about *social* transformation.

Other churches emphasize the importance of breathing out. If you attend these churches, it won't be long before you realize they want to impact the world in positive ways. They may organize themselves to speak out on issues of justice or poverty. Most Sundays, they're collecting canned goods for the community food pantry, winter jackets for the homeless, or sponsoring twelve-step groups. However, after a while you realize that preaching never speaks of the necessity of individuals having a life-changing encounter with Jesus Christ. Sin is rarely spoken of nor the need to make a decision to follow Christ. They have forgotten the *personal* transformation God longs to make in their hearts and lives. They do not seem to realize that the church not only must breathe out through service but also must breathe in through discipleship.

The healthy church is the congregation that combines *both* breathing in and breathing out. Such a community of faith sees no conflict between God transforming individuals within the church and God in turn using the church to change the world. Like inhaling and exhaling both come naturally to heart and lungs, so spiritual formation (inward looking) and ministry (outward looking) bring health to the body of Christ, the church.

Mere Ecclesiology unapologetically casts a communal vision, emphasizing God's plan for God's people. For all the differences between Africa and North America in the twenty-first century, the emphasis upon group identity is where we are witnessing

INTRODUCTION

the convergence of two worldviews. In a world made smaller by social media, jet travel, television, cell phones, and the internet, Africa's historic collective outlook carries huge appeal for North Americans born in the too-often isolating technological era. These young individuals are postmodern, inclusive, cooperative in how they learn and interact, and group-oriented in their thinking, a perspective that is also woven into life in much of sub-Saharan Africa. To be successful today, any model of how we "do church," whether in New York or Nairobi, must articulate itself within this communal framework. It is an energetic and optimistic perspective, longing to transform the here and now for Christ, together.

Finally, this book assumes an *intergenerational approach*. The results are in regarding churches where children, youth, and adults traipse off to separate corners to do their own thing, and the results are not pretty.[2] Rarely do youth who have grown up without meaningful relationships with adults in the community of faith succeed in themselves becoming engaged adult participants in church. Reaching their early twenties, they cast aside church like they would a worn shirt they've outgrown. As you read, constantly ask: *How can this idea be adopted in a way that children, teens, and adults can interact together?*

Mere Ecclesiology is an ideal text for membership classes, helping newcomers discover the church and their role in her mission. Likewise, longtime churchgoers will find it useful for small groups, to better understand the church's nature and purpose. To stimulate dialog, chapters conclude with discussion questions.

Let us now turn to part 1, "Breathing In." We begin by answering the question: "What is the church?"

---

2. See Powell and Clark, *Sticky Faith*.

Part One

Breathing In

1

The Church: God's Holy People

L'UNITÉ FAIT LA FORCE—UNITY is our strength. This national motto of the West African nation of Benin is a window into the larger sub-Saharan African worldview. Individuals are not unimportant, yet they find their deepest identity not alone but as part of a people.

This collective cultural value shows up in *pagne*, the colorful cotton material locally woven and sold in many places across Africa. One popular pattern shows cracked fingers, separated one from another, dry, lifeless, and empty. Next to them are hands, healthy and strong. All five fingers are connected, grasping pieces of gold that could only be gathered as they worked together. The Ivorian proverb reinforces a similar message: "You can't pick up a grain of rice with just one finger."

Modern individualism notwithstanding, historically, the United States has shared such a collective vision. Our tragic Civil War was fought from 1861–65 in part over the issue of whether we would be a single people. Prior to that conflict, it was common in writing to say: "The United States *are*." Now we say "The United States *is*." The Latin phrase *E pluribus unum*—one from many—appears on the seal of the nation.

This longing to be part of a people is no stranger to the pages of Scripture. Peter wrote to the Diaspora, believers scattered over five provinces of the Roman Empire: "But you are a chosen people, a royal priesthood, a holy nation, a people belonging to God, that you may declare the praises of him who called you out of darkness into his wonderful light" (1 Pet 2:9).

Part One: Breathing In

It is with the community of Christian faith—the holy people of God—that any study of how we can positively impact the world for Christ must begin. The church was here before any of us were born, and she will continue when we are gone. The words of the African saying—"I am because we are"—are no less fitting when it comes to matters of belief. So while we will later look at our individual response to Christ's call to follow him, we purposely begin with a more important concept than "me." Let us begin with "we."

What Is the Church?

One important way that the New Testament answers this question is: *We are God's holy people.* The *ecclesia*—the New Testament Greek word translated as "church"—stems from the assembly of free citizens in ancient Greek cities, including Ephesus (Acts 19:32, 39, 41).[1] Used in a Christian sense, it is a congregation or assembly of the faithful, or called out ones, from two words, *ek* (out) and *kaleō* (call).[2]

Jesus plays a special role in the Triune God as the founder of this people. Following Simon Peter's confession in Matthew 16:16 that Jesus was the "Messiah," the "Son of the living God," Jesus responded: "Now I say to you that you are Peter (which means 'rock'), and upon this rock I will build my church and the powers of hell will not conquer it" (Matt 16:18 NLT).

The "holy nation" described by Simon in 1 Peter 2:9 is pictured by Paul as the bride of Christ, washed in preparation for the bridegroom:

> Husbands, love your wives, just as Christ loved the church and gave himself up for her to make her holy, cleansing her by the washing with water through the word, and to present her to himself as a radiant church, without stain or wrinkle or any other blemish, but holy and blameless. (Eph 5:25–27)

---

1. Earle, *Word Meanings*, 16.
2. Ibid., 16.

Likewise, John's vision in Revelation 19:6–8 is of a bride adorned for her bridegroom, clothed in fine linen which is "bright and clean" (v. 8), symbolizing her purity. In this way, she has prepared herself for the "wedding of the Lamb" (v. 7).

Thomas Noble in *Holy Trinity, Holy People* picks up on this theme. Because Father, Son, and Holy Spirit are "essentially and inherently holy," he concludes: "The people of God are to be holy."[3] This echoes Peter's reaffirmation for the church of God's instructions in Leviticus 11:45 to the descendants of Abraham, Isaac, and Jacob, whom he had brought up from Egyptian slavery: "For it is written, 'Be holy, because I am holy'"(1 Pet 1:16). Peter gives these instructions as a father addressing his "obedient children" (v. 14) who must be different than the surrounding culture: "Do not conform" he warns "to the evil desires you had when you lived in ignorance" (v. 14). Holiness represents both purity and being set apart by God for a sacred task.

Unity and Reconciliation: Love in Action

Jesus emphasized love as the hallmark of the people of God: "By this everyone will know that you are my disciples, if you love one another" (John 13:35). One expression of love's priority in a holy community of faith is the commitment to unity. For this reason, Paul advised: "Make every effort to keep the unity of the Spirit through the bond of peace" (Eph 4:3). The chapter continues, casting a powerful vision of a body of believers centered upon Christ: "From him the whole body, joined and held together by every supporting ligament, grows and builds itself up in love, as each part does its work" (Eph 4:16).

Where contention holds sway, love withers. The apostle chastised the believers in Corinth for quarreling. Theirs was a congregation riven by competing parties, some claiming to follow Paul's teachings, others those of Apollos (1 Cor 3:1–5). At least once, the disagreement was so deep that they resorted to the local magistrate

---

3. Noble, *Holy Trinity, Holy People*, location 249.

to make a ruling, an action that Paul lambasted as beneath the dignity of the body of Christ and by implication a poor testimony to unbelievers (1 Cor 6:1–6).

Perhaps Paul emphasized unity because he knew from his own bitter experience how difficult it could be to achieve. When it was time for him and Barnabas to set out together on the second missionary journey, they failed to agree whether John Mark should come along. Barnabas's young protégé had abandoned them during the first missionary journey, and Paul apparently wasn't keen on the same thing happening again (Acts 13:13, 15:36–41). Luke explains in vv. 39–41: "They had such a sharp disagreement that they parted company. Barnabas took Mark and sailed for Cyprus, but Paul chose Silas and left, commended by the believers to the grace of the Lord. He went through Syria and Cilicia, strengthening the churches."

It is a tribute to both John Mark's ability to learn from his mistakes and Paul's willingness to forgive that in 2 Timothy 4:11 he writes to Timothy: "Only Luke is with me. Get Mark and bring him with you, because he is helpful to me in my ministry." Where unity has been torn apart, all is not lost. Reconciliation is always a possibility through Christ who has given the church the ministry of reconciliation (2 Cor 5:11–21).

Yet churches have underestimated the damage that strife among believers has inflicted upon the cause of Christ. We might euphemistically call it a "church plant," but the community knows a church split when it sees one. Shall a new church that came into being because of turmoil in the mother church be surprised when a few years down the road she herself is torn apart by acrimony?

John Wesley (1703–91) was no stranger to controversy. His actions did not always measure up to his own rhetoric. However, his sermon "Catholic Spirit" is still valued for the higher way to which it beckons us. Wesley asked:

> But although a difference in opinions or modes of worship may prevent an entire external union, yet need it prevent our union in affection? Though we cannot think alike, may we not love alike? May we not be of one heart,

though we are not of one opinion? Without all doubt, we may. Herein all the children of God may unite, notwithstanding these smaller differences.

Repeatedly he advised that if "thine heart is as my heart," there is but one thing to do: "Give me thy hand."

The old proverb is wise: "Don't make a mountain out of a molehill." Yet too often, are we bent on emphasizing the 10–20 percent of doctrine or practices where we diverge, never getting around to celebrating the 80–90 percent convergence in how we think and practice ministry? In the small Midwestern US town where I pastored, there were more than sixty churches in a county with a population of just over twenty-five thousand. In such an atmosphere, competition rather than collaboration was the order of the day. Sadly, I got caught up in the spirit of rivalry, helping found a separate ministerial association that further compromised our witness in the eyes of the community. It was a divisive act for which I later had to repent, yet the damage had been done. My actions, though well-intended, fell pitifully short of the winsome love among brothers and sisters that Jesus said must characterize his disciples.

Yet some churches have done better. My brother pastors a Wesleyan church in a small town on the East Coast of the United States. Before they were able to purchase their own land and construct a meeting place of their own, they were looking for a place to worship. The local Roman Catholic parish was happy to let them meet in their fellowship hall on Sunday afternoons. There was a time when such a gesture between Catholics and Protestants would have been unthinkable. Surely God is pleased when God's children support each other in such Christlike ways.

Summing It All Up

As the Beninese proverb teaches, unity is our strength. Followers of Jesus were never intended to go it alone. Who is the church? At her best, she is God's winsome, loving, united, holy people, a

Part One: Breathing In

vibrant community of Christian faith. *Yet how does the church corporately relate to individual believers on their faith journey?* This is the question of discipleship, and to this question we turn next.

Questions for Discussion

1. In 1 Peter 2:9, Peter describes the church as "a people belonging to God." If you were to ask an individual in your town to describe the church, would he or she be likely to use this description? Why or why not?
2. Unity is presented as one of the hallmarks of the people of God. Think of a time when division crept into a group of which you were a part, whether a club or at your place of employment. What caused the division? If the division was healed, how did that happen? What lessons can we learn in the church from these experiences in other areas of our lives?
3. Holiness is both purity and being set apart by God for a sacred task. How does being righteous help the church accomplish her mission? How might sin in the church hinder her from reaching God-given objectives?

2

Following Jesus, Together

AT THE CENTER OF Christianity is a cross. How strange is it that an ancient Roman instrument of torture and execution has become the most recognizable symbol in the world?

Theologians have pondered the cross for centuries yet still have not been able to fully explain its meaning. There are many verses in the New Testament that speak of the sacrificial death of Jesus of Nazareth that day long ago outside the walls of Jerusalem. Among these, some from Paul's letter to the Romans are among the best known: "But God demonstrates his own love for us in this: While we were still sinners, Christ died for us. Since we have now been justified by his blood, how much more shall we be saved from God's wrath through him!" (Rom 5:8–9).

We Were Still Sinners

To be a sinner is to sin, to disobey God either by doing what God forbids or refusing to do what God requires (1 John 3:4; Jas 4:17). The amazing thing about Romans 5:8 is that we deserved judgment but received grace, favor from heaven that we never earned. God could in anger have said to humanity after the disobedience of Adam and Eve: "You've made your bed. Now, lie in it." Yet from somewhere deep down in the great heart of this Three-in-One God, compassion welled up. A baby was born in a manger in Bethlehem, Immanuel, "God with us." Mary—a faithful young Jewish woman who had never had sex with a man—was confused. How could she be pregnant? What was this all about? Yet this miraculous conception had a purpose. The angel instructed Mary to name the child Jesus—"the Lord saves"—for "he will save his people from their sins" (Matt 1:21).

In the Old Testament, sin always required a sacrifice to atone, to make human beings once again at one with God. Reflecting on the book of Leviticus, the writer to the Hebrews observed: "In fact, the law requires that nearly everything be cleansed with blood, and without the shedding of blood there is no forgiveness" (Heb 9:22).

But God Demonstrated His Love

On the day Jesus died on the cross, that love was far from obvious for the men and women who had followed him for three years. The evidence seemed to point in the opposite direction, that God was demonstrating hatred toward Jesus. Did not Jesus himself, borrowing the words of Psalm 22:1, cry out: "'*Eloi, Eloi, lama sabacthani?*—which means, 'My God, my God, why have you forsaken me?'"

Anyone hung on a tree was considered cursed by God (Deut 21:23). That their Lord had died naked and brutally beaten could only have been interpreted as divine abandonment, or was it? As the disciples thought back over the time they had spent with their Lord, the cross finally made sense of some things that at the time were incomprehensible. They remembered the words of John the Baptist when Jesus came to be baptized in the river Jordan. Jesus' cousin John saw him coming, then announced loudly enough for all to hear: "Look, the Lamb of God, who takes away the sin of the world!" (John 1:29). As for Mary, the mother of Jesus, surely now the words of the angel made sense. Jesus himself had warned his disciples that he would die in Jerusalem and rise again after three days (Mark 8:31). Somehow, they had not been ready to hear those words. They filtered them out. Now, what had looked like hate and abandonment suddenly began to look like love. The death of Jesus was not in vain. It fulfilled a divine purpose and was motivated by God's love for us, for me! The innocent died so that the guilty might live.

We Have Now Been Justified

Sinners merit God's anger and punishment. Yet Paul says in Romans 5:9 that in Christ, we have been saved from God's wrath. We can be justified, forgiven, pardoned! Personal transformation always begins when our broken relationship with God is restored, thanks to what Jesus has done for us. Henry David Thoreau (1817–62) was a well-known writer and naturalist. As he neared death, his aunt came to visit him. She asked: "Have you made your peace with God?" Thoreau replied: "I didn't know that we had ever quarreled." Thoreau's response underscores the truth that we must be willing to admit that we have wronged God or else why seek God's forgiveness? Confession is a prerequisite for pardon. 1 John 1:8–9 teaches: "If we claim to be without sin, we deceive ourselves and the truth is not in us. If we confess our sins, he is faithful and just and will forgive us our sins and purify us from all unrighteousness."

From Pardon to Purity: Transformation God's Way

To be reconciled to God brings the blessing of adoption into God's family (Rom 8:15). Likewise, from that moment when we are reconciled, we become disciples of Jesus Christ, followers of his way. In *Mere Christianity*, C. S. Lewis taught that Christians are to be "little Christs."[1] This is not possible on our own, but our transformation into Christlike disciples begins immediately once we have been forgiven and agreed to let God direct us onto a new path.

This new mind-set—a willingness to forsake our sins, to let God change us since we are powerless to change ourselves—is called repentance. Placing our faith in Christ and what he has done for us at the cross, nothing short of a miracle transpires. Jesus calls this being "born again" (John 3:3), from which we get the terms "new birth" or "regeneration." Singer Keith Green recounts his own experience of deciding to follow Jesus, saying it was "like waking up from the longest dream." Paul insists that we become

---

1. Lewis, *Mere Christianity*, 169–70.

a "new creation" (2 Cor 5:17). With the Holy Spirit of God now living inside of us (1 Cor 6:18), God makes everything new.

The word that describes God's transforming work in our heart and life is *sanctification*. One meaning of the term is to be set apart for a sacred use. Some of the utensils used by the Hebrew priests in the tabernacle were to be sanctified, i.e., used only in the sacrifice of animals in the worship of God (Lev 8:10–11). In the same way, the follower of Jesus is to consider herself or himself as belonging totally to God. The disciple does not have the option to specify which parts of her or his life God may control. To be *entirely* sanctified means that all that we are and have is now under the lordship of Jesus Christ (Rom 12:1–2; 1 Thess 5:23–24). When God has all that we are, then God's holy presence, God's purity, and love fill us. Sin becomes distasteful as our attention focuses less and less on self-gratification and more and more on how we can love and serve others in the name of Jesus.

God Wants to Change the World, so He Changes Us First

At sixteen, I took my first job, working in the produce department of a grocery store. One night, my boss asked me to mop the floor of the back room. I did the job the best I knew how, but he was unsatisfied. When this went on for several nights, he finally asked me to demonstrate what I had been doing. "Greg," he said, "you'll never get the floor clean if you use a dirty mop dipped in dirty water. You'll just keep spreading the dirt around." The next night, I changed the dirty mop head for a clean one and frequently changed out the water. Success! The floor was clean and my boss was happy.

Looking at the church today, sometimes I think about mopping floors. We've understood that transformation of the world is not a distraction from the work of the gospel. It *is* gospel work. But unless we recognize that God must first transform us, then we risk just being dirty mops dipped in dirty water, spreading the dirt around and changing nothing. We cannot assume that just because individuals have been in the church all their lives that they have encountered the living Christ in a life-changing way! *Each of us must decide to follow Jesus.* Pardon and purity are available, but we must individually acknowledge our sin and make our peace with God through Christ (Rom 5:1). Paul challenges each of us:

> Therefore, I urge you, brothers, in view of God's mercy, to offer your bodies as living sacrifices, holy and pleasing to God—this is your spiritual act of worship. Do not conform any longer to the pattern of this world, but be transformed by the renewing of your mind. Then you will be able to test and approve what God's will is—his good, pleasing and perfect will." (Rom 12:1-2)

A prerequisite for transforming the world is God first transforming the church. God the Holy Spirit transforms us then we invite others to journey with us as we follow Jesus together. Christlike disciples make other Christlike disciples. God wants to change the world, so he changes us first.

Summing It All Up

The cross towers before us, a symbol of God's love and the sacrifice of Jesus so that we can be saved from our sins. In the cross, Jesus built a bridge between God and humanity, offering his own blood so that we can be forgiven and cleansed, set apart for God's own use. Justification and sanctification describe the radical transformation that God works in the lives of those who turn their back on their sins and decide to follow Jesus. As we become committed disciples—spurning sin and hungering for God—God uses us to make more disciples. In the next chapter, we'll examine the way that God uses worship to make disciples like Jesus, equipping them for service.

PART ONE: BREATHING IN

Questions for Discussion

1. What does the word "sin" mean? In your opinion, to what degree would most people today agree with this statement: "We are all sinners."

2. Sometimes we hear it said: "We are all God's children." Based on the information received in this chapter, would you agree or disagree with this contention? Why or why not?

3. Why is the cross of Jesus a vital part of how we think about God's forgiveness of our sins? Read Hebrews 13:12. How is the death of Jesus also related to sanctification?

4. What does the term "Christlike disciple" mean? Is the word "Christlike" a necessary adjective in relation to the noun "disciple" or is it redundant?

5. "The transformation of all creation begins with God changing us." Are you in agreement with this statement? If yes, why? If not, why not?

3

Beyond Self: Gathered to Worship

THE FIRST LINE OF Rick Warren's *Purpose Driven Life* may be its most profound: "It's not about you." Nothing that the church does together underscores this truth more than worship. When the people of God worship together, we are collectively caught up into the presence of the Eternal One who far surpasses our minuscule, temporal selves.

Sunday is sacred because—ever since the resurrection of Jesus on that first Easter morning—it has been the one time each week when collectively we set aside all distractions. It is on this day that we celebrate the risen Christ, focusing on God. The hymn by William Kethe calls us to forget self and directs our attention instead to divine royalty:

> Oh, worship the King, all glorious above,
> Oh, gratefully sing His pow'r and His love;
> Our Shield and Defender, the Ancient of Days,
> Pavilioned in splendor, and girded with praise.

It's All about the Three-in-One God

Note where the focus lies. Each person in the room—be it a small storefront with a low ceiling or a sanctuary in a high-vaulted cathedral—directs his or her attention heavenward. Self fades away in the bright light of God most high, God who is Three-in-One, Father, Son, and Holy Spirit. Like the prophet Isaiah, worship properly understood transports us beyond ourselves and takes us to another dimension where we catch a glimpse of the majesty of the King: "Holy, holy, holy is the LORD Almighty; the whole earth is full of his glory" (Isa 6:3).

This is the first and most important aspect of worship: *It is God-directed.* Worship entices us to bow our knee before God, funneling our attention not selfward but heavenward, celebrating the blessings of God with grateful hearts. In *Worship, Wonder, and Way,* Grant Zweigle sets the tone:

> In worship we turn our attention toward the divine other, the holy one in our midst, joining the eternal chorus of praise to the One we have come to know as Father, Son, and Holy Spirit. Worship is therefore one of the central ways the Christian church bears witness to the presence of the living God in our world today.[1]

As we lose ourselves in the divine majesty, something amazing and paradoxical transpires: *Steadfast refusal to focus upon ourselves in the end transforms us.*

We see this boomerang effect in Ephesians 3:14–21. Paul offers a prayer, yet it is not a hurried petition, a rote recitation. Rather, it is a prayer that breathes the essence of worship: "For this reason I kneel before the Father" (v. 14).

Paul takes on the role of worship leader, submitting as creature to Creator, bringing us collectively into the awesome presence of Almighty God. Importantly, this God is a tri-unity (Trinity) in nature and being. As Paul genuflects before the Father, he asks him to strengthen our "inner selves" through "the Spirit" (v. 16). He invites Christ himself to live in our hearts "through faith" (v. 17). Oh, the mystery of the Three-in-One God! And not surprisingly, where this Trinitarian God abides, love is never far away: "I ask that you'll have the power to grasp love's width and length, height and depth, together with all believers. I ask that you'll know the love of Christ that is beyond knowledge so that you will be filled entirely with the fullness of God" (v. 18–19). If there was any doubt about

---

1. Zweigle, *Worship, Wonder, and Way,* 37.

the corporate setting of Paul's prayer, it evaporates in v. 21: "Glory to him in the church and in Christ Jesus for all generations, forever and always. Amen." The prayer underscores what God wants to do in our hearts together as we unite them in worship and prayer.

Music as Worship

Followers of Christ have inherited from the Hebrew people the Psalter, a magnificent book of Psalms (or songs) written by David and various others. The Psalms set the tone for our praise: "I rejoiced with those who said to me, 'Let us go to the house of the LORD'" (Ps 122:1).

Turning to the New Testament, Paul promoted the use of psalms, hymns, and spiritual songs as a way to "sing and make music from your heart to the Lord" (Eph 5:19). Likewise, the psalmist encouraged worshippers to play a variety of instruments of their day, including the lute, lyre, the ram's horn, and the cymbals (Ps 150:3–5). By extension, musicians today use contemporary tools to "burst into jubilant song with music" (Ps 98:4b), whether it be keyboards, the djembe, drums, guitars, trumpets, saxophones, violins, clarinets, or a dozen other instruments. A hundred-voice choir, a praise team, a band, or the mass of people gathered who join their voices together, all use the musical talent God has liberally sprinkled around. Our responsibility and joy is to discover those talents and to give them back to the Lord for God's glory.

Scripture, Prayer, and Response

Besides music, in later chapters we will talk about preaching, the Eucharist (the Lord's Supper), and baptism. These are important elements of worship, but there are more. Historically, the church has included four times during worship for the out-loud reading of Bible portions by individuals capable of reading the Scriptures with clarity and feeling. Men and women, youth and children should all be part of the team of Scripture readers on a rotating

Part One: Breathing In

basis, each worship service containing the reading of two Old Testament passages and two New Testament passages. For the Old Testament, this often includes a reading from the Prophets and the Psalms, whereas the New Testament readings are selections from the Gospels and the Epistles. The *Revised Common Lectionary* is one popular guide that designates the readings for each Sunday of the year.

Worship is not passive; it is participatory. Reciting the Lord's Prayer or the Apostles' Creed are common ways that worship leaders elicit the participation of everyone present. Further, there are responses that the congregation voices together, sometimes including snippets of Scripture, other times simple formulas that keep the congregation focused. Following the reading of Scripture, the reader often will say: "This is the word of the Lord," to which the people respond: "Thanks be to God." At the close of the worship service, pastors or other leaders will invite the congregation to recite "The Grace," adapted from 2 Corinthians 13:14:

> May the grace of our Lord Jesus Christ,
> and the love of God,
> and the fellowship of the Holy Spirit
> be with us all,
> now and evermore.
> Amen.

Prayer is another way for worshippers to respond. Whether the kneeling bench is directly in front of participants or down in front (an "altar"), the leaders invite those gathered to join in times of prayer. The pastoral prayer in many Christian traditions allows the shepherd a special moment when she or he brings the people before God, praying aloud for their needs, the forgiveness of sins and God's blessings and protection, even as those kneeling pray softly or silently. Church leaders may anoint with oil those who are sick (Jas 5:14–15), praying for their healing in the name of Jesus.

Response can go far beyond words to involving our entire body in worship. Many in West Africa cannot stay seated as the djembe sets the cadence for dancing. Joy is written on many a face as worshippers sway to the music, some stepping out into the aisles, inviting others to join them in a train of worship dancers. A jubilant worship chorus in Côte d'Ivoire celebrates the royal dance in 2 Samuel 6:14, urging: "David was a great king, and he got up to dance!" Likewise, churches in North America will sometimes involve a small troupe of worship dancers who through their kinesthetic gifts bring praise to God.

The genius of the people of God gathered to worship is variety. You may not be able to carry a tune and may have two left feet. Still, everyone can contribute something, even if it's small. The giving of tithes (10 percent of income) and offerings (any amount) by those gathered is another way to worship, dropping our monetary gift in the offering plate or—as is common in many African nations—walking or dancing up front to place coins or bills in a basket. In this way, today's followers of Christ follow a tradition dating to the Old Testament Levites who lived on the gifts of God's people (Num 18:21). In the New Testament, offerings were a way to support pastors (1 Cor 9:1–11) or provide relief to the poor (2 Cor 8:1–15). Today, tithes and offerings are used to support these and a variety of other ministries in service to the community.

Summing It All Up

Worship is the joyous weekly celebration of the Triune God. Likewise, it is the heartfelt corporate thanksgiving of God's people for heaven's blessings. More than at any other time during the week, Sunday morning is the visible manifestation of our unity in Christ, a winsome and holy moment that invites one and all into the transforming presence of the Holy Spirit. Let us turn in the next chapter to the preaching of God's Word, a key moment in worship.

Questions for Discussion

1. Some churches offer worship services on Saturday evening in addition to traditional Sunday morning worship. Why

Part One: Breathing In

do churches continue to emphasize Sunday morning as the church's primary gathering time?

2. Does your church have an altar? If yes, at what points during the worship service do people come to kneel? What would be the reaction of the people if the altar were suddenly removed?

3. Giving of our tithes and offerings is a corporate act of worship. How might the convenience of giving online (or through our cell phones) be incorporated into the worship service?

4. Discuss worship in your own local church setting. In what ways are people encouraged to use their body to worship God?

4

Preach It!

PREACHERS TODAY GET A bad rap. "Don't preach at me" figures on the list of most popular comebacks, along with "Stop judging me." In modern usage, to preach at someone is to set oneself up as superior, to condescendingly render a verdict on another's behavior. It is the pop star Madonna pleading with her father: "Papa, don't preach."

Yet preaching wasn't always devalued. There was a time when "preacher" was a term of endearment, a little less formal than "reverend" but respectful nonetheless. As recently as 1996 in the film *The Preacher's Wife*, Courtney Vance portrayed Reverend Henry Biggs, an African American pastor who—while insensitive to his wife's needs—was nevertheless committed to his work, selflessly serving the members of his inner-city flock. Being a preacher was cool.

So if the term "preacher" has lately fallen on hard times, why do the people of God continue to use it? To answer this question, let's briefly look at what the New Testament has to say about preaching and its importance.

John and Jesus, the Preaching Cousins

A good place to begin is with the cousins, John and Jesus. John went into the wilderness and took up a simple lifestyle, wearing clothes made of camel's hair and eating locusts and wild honey (Matt 3:4). People streamed to John and he baptized them with water as a sign of their abandoning their sinful ways. Yet the baptizing followed preaching. We don't have a lot of detail about what John preached, but it wasn't for the faint of heart. He urged people to produce good fruit, proof of their changed ways. He called religious leaders "snakes" (Matt 3:7), demanded that tax collectors not collect more than they were required, and warned soldiers not to accuse people falsely or to extort money. Instead, he told them to be content with their salary (Luke 3:7–14). John's boldness in preaching knew no social boundaries, and he paid for his boldness with his head (Matt 14:1–12).

Yet John was merely a warm-up act for the main attraction. About Jesus of Nazareth, John testified: "He must become greater and greater, and I must become less and less" (John 3:30 NLT). Filled with the Holy Spirit, Jesus passed his test in the wilderness, resisting the temptations of the devil (Matt 4:1–11). After this testing, what did Jesus do? He immediately began to preach: "Repent, for the kingdom of heaven has come near" (4:17). In fact, the kingdom of heaven and the parables Jesus drew from everyday life became the staple of his magnetic preaching. Just before returning to heaven, Jesus commanded his disciples to preach the gospel (literally, "good news") to all creation (Mark 16:15). We preach because it is the command of our Lord to do so.

Peter and Paul: Preaching with the Cross and the Resurrection at the Center

The book of Acts records the obedience of the apostles to Jesus' command. When the Holy Spirit fell at Pentecost—a Jewish feast held annually in Jerusalem—Peter rose and preached a powerful message, climaxing with his explanation of the sacrifice of Jesus on the cross and Jesus' resurrection (Acts 2:31–36). By raising Jesus from the dead, God made him both "Lord and Christ" (2:36). What is to be our response to so great a vindication by God of this Jesus? Luke summarizes Peter's words: "With many other words he warned them; and he pleaded with them, 'Save yourselves from this corrupt generation'" (Acts 2:41). Many were cut to the heart, and three thousand were baptized that day in response.

Preach It!

Like Peter, Paul believed that preaching was a powerful tool that God uses to capture the attention of listeners. Romans 10:14–15 speaks of those who are sent by the church. And what is their task? They are to preach:

> How, then, can they call on the one they have not believed in? And how can they believe in the one of whom they have not heard? And how can they hear without someone preaching to them? And how can anyone preach unless they are sent? As it is written: "How beautiful are the feet of those who bring good news!"

The content of the preaching becomes clearer in 1 Corinthians 1. Paul insists: "For the message of the cross is foolishness to those who are perishing, but to us who are being saved it is the power of God" (1 Cor 1:18). For Paul, the death of Christ on a cross was the ultimate demonstration of the love of God: "But God demonstrates his own love for us in this: While we were still sinners, Christ died for us" (Rom 5:8). To the sacrifice of Christ, Paul later in his letter adds the miracle of the resurrection: "And if Christ has not been raised our preaching is useless and so is your faith" (1 Cor 15:14). The obedience of death on a cross was followed by God "highly exalting him" (Phil 2:9). Though some mocked him, Paul never abandoned his insistence that Jesus was alive and would one day come again as judge (Acts 17:29–34). It was not a dead Jesus but the living Christ who appeared to Paul on the road to Damascus and commissioned him as the apostle to preach to the Gentiles (Acts 26:15–18).

In the preaching of Peter and Paul, we realize that the cross and the empty tomb were not an add-on to the message shared by the early church. The theme of suffering and victory was at the center of their proclamation. Can this still be said of preaching in our time?

Part One: Breathing In

Preaching and Sacraments Belong Together

In later chapters, we will learn more about the meaning and practice of the Eucharist (Lord's Supper) and baptism. Together, many churches refer to these two faith-strengthening practices as the sacraments. But it may be asked: How are preaching and the celebration of sacraments related? John Stott explains:

> Both quicken our faith in Christ. Both enable us to feed on Christ in our hearts. The major difference between them is that the message of the one is directed to the eye, and the message of the other to the ear. So the sacraments need the Word to interpret them. The ministry of Word and sacrament is a single ministry, the Word proclaiming, and the sacraments dramatizing, God's promises. Yet the Word is primary, since without it the sign becomes dark in meaning, if not actually dumb.[1]

While Stott's conclusion that preaching is "primary" can be debated, the proclamation of the Word as part of the worship service is without doubt an ancient practice of the people of God. Already in the book of Acts, the Apostle Paul engaged informal discourse with believers and nonbelievers (Acts 20:11, 24:26), in the former case in the context of breaking bread, a reference to the Lord's Supper. Justin Martyr (AD 100–165) noted in his *First Apology* that on Sunday Christians came together to—among other things—hear a sermon by the bishop.[2] Later, the *Westminster Shorter Catechism*, written in the 1640s, taught that "preaching of the word" is a means of "convincing and converting sinners" and "building them up in holiness."[3]

When we come together to worship, the preaching of the Word of God is a crucial aspect of what we do. Preaching is the means that God uses to awaken faith in the hearts of unbelievers (Rom 10:17). It is also a means of grace, one way among others that God uses to strengthen the faith of believers. This vital aspect

---

1. Stott, *Between Two Worlds*, 114.
2. "Homily," New Advent Catholic Encyclopedia.
3. The *Westminster Shorter Catechism* can be found at reformed.org.

of preaching is evidenced by Paul's advice to Timothy to devote himself to the public reading of Scripture, to teaching, and to preaching (1 Tim 4:14).

In every generation, we believe that God calls individuals—both women and men (Acts 2:18, Rom 16:3, 7, Gal. 3:28)—to the ministry of preaching. Each generation needs a new wave of preachers, spokespersons for God who—in the power of the Holy Spirit—clothe the truth of the gospel of Christ in the idiom of our time, language that touches listeners. God needs our best and brightest to prepare themselves spiritually and educationally for this difficult and sacred task.

Like the celebration of the Lord's Supper and the practice of baptism, God uses preaching to form us in the image of Christ, to help us follow Jesus even more closely. Rather than prioritizing either preaching or sacraments as more important, we should recognize that God uses them *both* as ways to transform us, making us more and more like Jesus.

Summing It All Up

St. Francis of Assisi advised: "Preach the gospel at all times and when necessary use words." Our actions commend Christ to others, and to our actions are added the inspired commentary on Scripture called preaching, anointed by the Holy Spirit. Let us turn next in greater detail to the sacraments, the practices of Eucharist (the Lord's Supper) and baptism.

Questions for Discussion

1. What feelings does the word "preacher" evoke for you? Does preaching belong only in a church building or does it have a place on the streets or in other public locations?
2. How much of a worship service should be given to preaching? Does it matter whether preaching comes before the celebration of the Lord's Supper or after?

Part One: Breathing In

3. Think about the various styles of preachers that you've heard. What kind of preaching for you is most helpful? Why?

4. The chapter spoke of preaching about the cross and the resurrection of Jesus. Do you agree that these should be a central part of preaching? If so, what role should the Old Testament and other New Testament ideas play in the overall preaching program of the church?

5. Do you agree that both preaching and the sacraments can be transformational? If so, exactly how do they transform us individually and as the church corporately?

5

Come to the Table

PEOPLE WERE ASKING QUESTIONS. Their pastor was new and—so far—had celebrated communion every Sunday, something they'd never done before, so they decided to ask him about it. "Don't you think it will become routine if we do this together *every week*?" The pastor was quiet for a minute, then posed a question of his own. "Do you think God is in heaven looking down at us and saying, 'Stop it, people! Don't do that so much!'" His listeners laughed; they took his point. The next Sunday, they gladly went forward during communion time.

Sacraments are dramatic rites/ceremonies—or to use Augustine's term, "visible words"—modeled by Jesus and instituted by him that he intended the people of God to practice as well. In the next chapter, we will consider another sacrament, that of baptism. Baptism is the initiation that marks off individuals as belonging to the people of God, the church. In this chapter, we will examine the sacrament called "Eucharist," sometimes given the name "Holy Communion," "communion," or the "Lord's Supper."

The term "Eucharist" comes from the Greek verb *eucharisto*, meaning to "give thanks." The night before his crucifixion, Jesus took bread and wine and *gave thanks* for them before giving them to his disciples (Matt 26:27, Luke 22:19; see also 1 Cor 11:24). Luke 22:14–23 picks up the story:

> When the hour came, Jesus and his apostles reclined at the table. And he said to them, "I have eagerly desired to eat this Passover with you before I suffer. For I tell you, I

will not eat it again until it finds fulfillment in the kingdom of God."

After taking the cup, he gave thanks and said, "Take this and divide it among you. For I tell you I will not drink again from the fruit of the vine until the kingdom of God comes."

And he took bread, gave thanks and broke it, and gave it to them, saying, "This is my body given for you; do this in remembrance of me."

In the same way, after the supper he took the cup, saying, "This cup is the new covenant in my blood, which is poured out for you. But the hand of him who is going to betray me is with mine on the table. The Son of Man will go as it has been decreed. But woe to that man who betrays him!" They began to question among themselves which of them it might be who would do this.

Meaning of the Eucharist

The context of this ritual is important. Jesus and his disciples were celebrating the Passover. This annual Jewish feast commemorated the miraculous and hurried exit of the Hebrew slaves from Egypt. Particularly, it memorialized the last of the ten plagues that God had visited upon Pharaoh and the Egyptians, the LORD killing the firstborn Egyptian sons (see Exod 11–12). Each Hebrew household was to sacrifice a lamb without blemish. Next, they were to sprinkle some of its blood on the sides and tops of the doorframes. Finally, they were to roast the meat of the lamb, accompanied with bitter herbs and bread without yeast. When the LORD saw the blood on the doorposts, he would "pass over" that house, leaving all its inhabitants untouched (Exod 12:13).

It is only in retrospect and through the eyes of faith that we can see how Jesus became the spotless Lamb of God slain for the sins of the world (John 1:29; Rev 5:12). He was the fulfillment of the old covenant—or agreement between God and God's people—and now on the eve of his death, Jesus introduced a new covenant. Now he anticipated his crucifixion at Golgotha the next day. He broke the bread and called it a symbol of his broken body. Likewise, the wine in the cup symbolized for Jesus the blood that he would shed on the cross. In 1 Corinthians 11:23–26, Paul adds two other important aspects:

> For I received from the Lord what I also passed on to you: The Lord Jesus, on the night he was betrayed, took bread, and when he had given thanks, he broke it and said, "This is my body, which is for you; do this in remembrance of me." In the same way, after supper he took the cup, saying, "This cup is the new covenant in my blood; do this, whenever you drink it, in remembrance of me." For whenever you eat this bread and drink this cup, you proclaim the Lord's death until he comes.

Here we see that there is no prescribed frequency for celebrating the Eucharist. Paul simply says "whenever." (However, for the early church, this quickly became a weekly observance.) Second, he talks about the historical time frame for celebrating this sacrament. It began when Jesus instituted it "the night he was betrayed" and it is to be practiced "until he comes."

What the Eucharist Is Not

It may help us to first look at a few misconceptions about the Eucharist. To do so, let us ask the question: *What is the Eucharist not?*

It Is Not a Test

In Corinth, some were getting drunk on the wine during the *agape*, a common meal shared by the believers preliminary to the Eucharist. They gorged themselves while others went hungry (1 Cor 11:21). Paul was angry and warned them that if this abuse continued, even more might become weak, sick, or "fall asleep" (1 Cor 11:30). This is the context for Paul's warning not to eat the bread or drink the cup in an "unworthy manner." Well-meaning Christians have torn this out of context, scaring faithful believers away from the Lord's Table, warning them to make sure they are "worthy" before partaking. One Liberian pastor told of hearing a preacher say that each time a communicant received the bread unworthily, it would stay in his stomach and eventually clog up the digestive system, causing death. Such a misconception makes of what should be a joyous celebration an ordeal, defined by *Merriam-Webster's Online Dictionary* as "a primitive means used to determine guilt or innocence by submitting the accused to dangerous or painful tests believed to be under supernatural control." Let's face it: If worthiness—understood as us meriting Christ's sacrifice—was a condition for receiving the Eucharist, no one would take it. We come to the table not because we are worthy, but because Christ is worthy, and he extends a winsome invitation. Shall we ignore the feast he has spread for us?

It Is Not a Reward for Exemplary Churchmanship

The Eucharist must not be tied to other practices such as the giving of tithes and offerings or regular attendance. Some have reported churches in Africa that issue to her members attendance and tithing cards that ushers fill out each week. In this scenario, only those who pass a certain minimal standard are admitted to the Eucharist. Is this what Jesus had in mind when he said that his burden was light and his yoke easy (Matt 11:29)? Did he not instead say: "Come to me, all you who are weary and burdened, and I will give you rest" (Matt 11:28)? Nothing says "Come to me" like the Lord's Supper. Shall we turn away from his Table those who hunger and thirst for righteousness?

It Is Not a Magical Ceremony with Magical Substances

Whenever spiritual truths are made concrete by visible objects, there is the danger that the visible objects become the focus of our attention rather than the invisible One to whom the objects point. King Hezekiah, as a sign of his loyalty to Yahweh, was forced to break into pieces the bronze snake that Moses had made in the wilderness at God's direction as a remedy for the snakebites from the serpents God had sent into the camp (Num 21:9; 2 Kgs 18:14). In the same way, we should ascribe no inherent power to bread or wine even if sometimes we sing hymns such as "There is power in the blood." We believe there is power not in the blood as such but in Jesus who shed his blood. (For the same reason, we reject the use of "Holy Water" as if the water in itself contains power.) We must always focus our attention on the One who lies behind the sign and not put our faith in the efficacy of the symbol. Otherwise, like the ancient Israelites, we are taking a magical approach to the things of God. The belief in transubstantiation—that the bread and wine become the actual body and blood of Christ after the priest pronounces certain words—may lend itself to a magical approach to the sacraments. It is a too literal application of the words of Jesus, "This is my body" or "This is my blood." Symbols should not be confused with the reality behind the symbols.

What the Eucharist Is

We've looked at a few things that the Eucharist is not. We are ready to ask the question: *So what exactly is the Eucharist?*

The Eucharist Is Remembering the Sacrifice of Christ for Us

Jesus invited his disciples to eat the bread and drink the wine as a way of remembering his sacrifice. He said: "Do this in remembrance of me." Too often, the celebration of Holy Communion resembles a funeral. Yet should not remembering the sacrifice of Christ on our behalf fill us with joy, not sorrow? Smiling and dancing—expressions of thanksgiving—may be more appropriate responses at the Lord's Table than long faces and hunched shoulders.

Part One: Breathing In

The Lord's Supper Is a Celebration of Solidarity with Brothers and Sisters in Christ

Acts 2:46–47 paints a picture of a united church:

> Every day they continued to meet together in the temple courts. They broke bread in their homes and ate together with glad and sincere hearts, praising God and enjoying the favor of all the people. And the Lord added to their number daily those who were being saved.

"Breaking bread" may refer to the *agape* or the Eucharist, perhaps to both. In any case, it's clear that table fellowship created oneness. Because communion celebrates the oneness of the body of Christ, it is always appropriate for visitors from any Christian community of faith to participate, whether or not they are members of the local congregation or denomination where the Lord's Supper is being celebrated on that particular occasion. This is known as "open communion."

The Eucharist Is a Means of Grace

John Wesley (1703–91) in his sermon "The Means of Grace," defined "means of grace" as the "ordinary channels whereby he [God] might convey to men, preventing, justifying, or sanctifying grace." He identified the means of grace as prayer, Bible reading, and "receiving the Lord's Supper, eating bread and drinking wine in remembrance of him."

Preventing (or prevenient) grace is the drawing activity of the Holy Spirit, attracting people to Christ (John 6:44, 12:32). Justifying grace is a synonym for pardon or forgiveness of sins. What does this tell us as related to the Lord's Supper? In the Wesleyan understanding of communion, we believe that the Holy Spirit is present at the sacrament, drawing people—believers and nonbelievers—to God. Therefore, for the nonbeliever, being drawn to the table and taking Holy Communion could be their *first act of faith*, first steps in a lifelong journey of discipleship. Similarly, for the prodigal son or daughter, it may be the moment when they make their way home to God. Because of this, we must be careful not to set up a barrier in one's path by impeding access to the table for the sake of our ecclesiology, of who's "in" and who's "out." Jesus says to one and all: "Come!" One can always follow up with people later, inquiring about their faith and what God is doing in their lives. Those who are unbaptized can be encouraged to enroll in baptism classes, to formally identify with the people of God. One thing is clear: The Lord's Supper is never the time to push away seekers who are drawing closer to Christ.

A father had long prayed for his son who for years had wanted nothing to do with the church. One Sunday, the son and his girlfriend finally came to worship. The father saw the beginning of God's answer to his prayers. He was thrilled to see his son at church but was afraid of how he might react during the celebration of Holy Communion at the end of the service. Would he be turned away? What would the pastor say? Much to his relief, the Holy Spirit seemed to be guiding the pastor's choice of words. Besides faithful believers, the pastor invited all who wanted to follow Christ for the first time to come to the table. He added that those who had been far away were also welcome to make this celebration of the Eucharist their joyous homecoming. Eagerly, the wayward son and his girlfriend both joined the line. They happily received the bread and drank the cup presented to them with the words: "The body of our Lord, broken for you . . . the blood of our Lord, shed for you." Surely this exemplifies Jesus's intent as recorded in Revelation 22:17: "The Spirit and the bride say, 'Come!' And let the one who hears say, 'Come!' Let the one who is thirsty come; and let the one who wishes take the free gift of the water of life."

At the Lord's Supper, an unbeliever may respond to this universal call, resulting in saving faith. Likewise, the wanderer may return to the fold. Finally, the committed follower will be strengthened in his or her faith, empowered for continued service. All three of these categories of individuals—full of faith, though in various locations on their spiritual journey—are God's "faithful people" as described in a Eucharistic hymn by Charles Wesley:

> O the depth of love Divine,
> Th'unfathomable grace!
> Who shall say how bread and wine
> God into man conveys!
> *How* the bread his flesh impart
> How the wine transmits His blood
> Fills his faithful people's hearts
> With all the life of God!

Summing It All Up

John Wesley spoke of the "duty of constant communion." With due respect to Methodism's cofounder, he got this title wrong. Communion, Mr. Wesley, is no duty, no burden. Rather, it is a joy, a celebration of the good things of God given to us in Christ. Yet the Eucharist—though vital—is only one of the sacraments. Baptism is also vital, and it is to this practice that we turn in the next chapter.

Questions for Discussion

1. Have you ever refrained from taking the Lord's Supper because you felt "unworthy"? Does understanding the Eucharist as a "means of grace" change whether you might sometimes abstain?

2. What are the three categories of people who are welcome to the table of the Lord?

3. Based on the discussion in question 2, at what age may an individual receive Holy Communion?

4. What advice is given regarding those who receive communion but are unbaptized?

5. Have you ever participated in a Christian worship service where the Eucharist was celebrated but where the table was in some way "fenced off"? Tell of your experience. What is meant by "open communion" and what are its advantages?

6

Baptism: Joining God's People

WEST AFRICA HAS MANY people groups. Different tribes "mark off" their babies with distinctive scars. One of my adult students, Francis, had an inch-long scar on his right cheek, just under his eye. During a break in class, I asked him about it. "This mark shows that I belong to my people," he explained.

This practice may seem strange to those born in a Western setting, though with the rise of tattoos, perhaps less strange than in days gone by. Yet for any student of the Bible, African scarification immediately evokes how God marked off the ancient male Israelites as God's own. Genesis 17:23–27 explains:

> On that very day Abraham took his son Ishmael and all those born in his household or bought with his money, every male in his household, and circumcised them, as God told him. Abraham was ninety-nine years old when he was circumcised, and his son Ishmael was thirteen; Abraham and his son Ishmael were both circumcised on that very day. And every male in Abraham's household, including those born in his household or bought from a foreigner, was circumcised with him.

For both Africans and ancient Jews, personal identity evokes "we" more than "me." The people to whom I belong is of first and overriding importance. My story is important only as it is caught up in the larger story of my people.

BAPTISM: JOINING GOD'S PEOPLE

The Old Testament People of God

The Old Testament takes this concept of group solidarity and goes one step further. Not only is the individual enfolded into the story of his or her people—the priority of "we" over "me"—but the people's story in turn is caught up in a much bigger story, the Story of God. In a land infested with idols to false gods, the prophet Jeremiah warned of a coming exile, but gave the hope of a people who would be reconstituted one day:

> They will be my people, and I will be their God. I will give them singleness of heart and action, so that they will always fear me and that all will then go well for them and for their children after them. (Jer 32:38–39)

They will be my people, and I will be their God. This is the language of covenant, a solemn agreement between Yahweh and the people of God. Isaiah 49:6 is just one of a constellation of Old Testament passages that speak of Israel as a "light for the Gentiles." They were to be a holy people, an example to the nations. Isaiah 56:6 speaks of "foreigners" who would come to Jerusalem, the "holy mountain," to pray and make sacrifices to God. God's people were to be a righteous, winsome, countercultural presence in the world, attracting even foreigners like a magnet to worship the one true God in the beauty of holiness.

The New Testament People of God

Old Testament passages like those in Isaiah are a bridge to the New Testament. In the New Testament, the people of God is no longer defined as blood descendants of Abraham. Rather, the people of God is comprised of anyone—Jew or Gentile—who are persons of the new covenant, the "new and living way" to God opened up through the sacrificial death of Christ (Heb 10:20). These individuals of the new covenant, this people of God, is the church.

Just as the ancient Jews "marked off" their male children through the rite of circumcision, so the new people of God, the church, marks off its young through a rite, that of water baptism. This replacement of circumcision by baptism is most explicit in the words of Paul in Colossians 2:9–12:

> For in Christ all the fullness of the Deity lives in bodily form, and in Christ you have been brought to fullness. He is the head over every power and authority. In him you were also circumcised with a circumcision not performed by human hands. Your whole self ruled by the flesh was put off when you were circumcised by Christ, having been buried with him in baptism, in which you were also raised with him through your faith in the working of God, who raised him from the dead.

When the church evangelizes in communities largely untouched by the gospel, many adults who come to Christ will not have had the blessing of growing up in a Christian home. In the United States, this is becoming more common. In some states, church attendance on a Sunday morning involves less than 10 percent of the population. Converts in such a context are unlikely to have a Christian heritage and therefore unlikely to have been baptized younger in life. So, though older, they have never been initiated into the people of God. They, too, will pass through the door of water baptism into the household of faith, like the Ethiopian eunuch Philip baptized in the desert (Acts 8:26–40).

As for the child baptized as an infant, they should receive later at a time when they can understand (traditionally around age twelve) instruction in the meaning of their baptism and what it signifies to belong to the people of God. It is then—at the time some call "confirmation"—that they can affirm Christian faith as their own. By doing so, they acknowledge what their parents by proxy accomplished when they presented them as babies for baptism. Confirmation means saying: "From the start, my parents always intended me to follow Christ, to be part of God's people. Now, I openly acknowledge that these are my people, that Jesus is my Savior, and that I am his follower."

Like in many African cultures, so in the Christian family, the "we" precedes the "me." This vital progression from "the faith of my family" to "my faith, too" is found in Paul's words to Timothy: "I am reminded of your sincere faith, which first lived in your grandmother Lois and in your mother Eunice and, I am persuaded, now lives in you also" (2 Tim 1:5).

Across Africa, there is an influx of converts to Christian faith. In a context where most are exiting African traditional religions, it is normal that most who are baptized are older. Yet as time goes by, the practice of baptism of those who are infants or young children is likely to increase, as portrayed in the book of Acts when entire families were baptized together (Acts 2:37–41; 16:33). Likewise, as believers in the West shift from the "Jesus and me" perspective to that of "Jesus and we," the frequency of baptizing the young will surely grow. In any case, there is one baptism, not two (Eph 4:5). Baptism remains the once-in-a-lifetime sacrament (literally, "visible word") of initiation into the people of God, though it may be performed very early or later in life, depending upon the circumstances.

Summing It All Up

Whether the sacrament of baptism is administered to an infant who later is confirmed or (alternatively) to an adult candidate, the people of God are the people of the covenant established by the blood of Christ (Luke 22:20). The "marking off" of baptism is an initiation into that holy people, at whatever age it occurs. It is an acknowledgment of the priority of who we are together, that the people of God predated me and they will continue when I am gone. I am a chapter in a book, an important chapter, to be sure, but the book is a story of "we" with many chapters. Through baptism, I have been caught up in this bigger, divine, corporate story, the story of God and God's people.

Yet baptism is not an end; it is a beginning. Together, the people of God participate in disciplines that are part of the "breathing in" of spiritual respiration. Two of these practices are prayer and fasting. It is to these crucial disciplines that we now turn our attention.

Part One: Breathing In

Questions for Discussion

1. Most Christian churches require individuals to be baptized before they can join church membership. Why do you think this is a requirement?
2. Baptism is the sacrament of initiation into the people of God. What could parents who present their young children for baptism do so that when older the child will be able to look back at their baptism?
3. A pastor was once asked: "Can a person be re-baptized?" She replied: "Can a person be re-circumcised?" Explain the logic behind the pastor's response.
4. Historically, many churches have allowed baptism by immersion, pouring, or sprinkling. In what situations might one mode of baptism be preferable over another?
5. The author views baptism as an expression of solidarity, of the priority of "we" over "me" in the Story of God. Do you agree? Why or why not?

7

Prayer and Fasting

CORRIE TEN BOOM ONCE asked: "Is prayer your steering wheel or your spare tire?" In our more honest moments, we might admit that too much of our praying is done in times of distress; the rest of the time, we do what we want without consulting God. Despite our shortcomings, the ideal remains before our eyes. Across the centuries, followers of Christ have practiced prayer and fasting both individually and corporately. Scripture and the church view this twin practice as essential to growing in grace and deepening one's relationship with God. Prayer and fasting are a vital part of spiritual respiration, a "breathing in" of intimacy with God that allows us to "breathe out" in service to the world.

Prayer, a Discipline of the Spirit

Prayer is communication with God. Like any type of communication, prayer involves both *sending* and *receiving*. As humans, we speak to God; in turn, God will speak to us if we are tuned in to God's voice.

Often we turn to God during difficult times. The Lord does not forbid us to do so. (Sometimes, we need a "spare tire"!) In fact, Scripture encourages us to pray during times of distress. "Do not be anxious about anything," says the Apostle Paul, "but in every situation, by prayer and petition, with thanksgiving, present your requests to God. And the peace of God, which transcends all understanding, will guard your hearts and your minds in Christ Jesus" (Phil 4:6–7). Likewise, prayers of intercession—praying for someone else—are welcome to God. Writing to Philemon, Paul notes: "I always thank my God as I remember you in my prayers" (Phlm 1:4). Saint Augustine credited the fervent prayers of his mother, Monica, on his behalf for his eventually coming to Christ as a young man.

Prayer is also listening to God. In John 10, Jesus compares himself to a shepherd and his followers to sheep, observing: "My sheep listen to my voice; I know them, and they follow me" (10:27). Through prayer, we sense God's deep love for us. We are reminded that God is our Father and that we are God's children.

Discerning between the voice of God and the voice of the devil is a critical skill. As a general rule, if our inner voice is one of accusation, then we can know such a voice does not come from God. Revelation 12:10 describes the devil as "the accuser of our brothers and sisters, who accuses them before our God day and night." On the other hand, the Holy Spirit will gently correct believers, convicting us of sin when we act contrary to the light of God (John 16:8; 1 John 1:5–7). Some describe this common phenomenon as being "checked in my spirit," a sudden sense of discomfort when taking part in an inadvisable activity or speaking in a way not pleasing to God. This is the voice of the Lord, warning us away from a dangerous course of action.

As Corrie ten Boom suggests, prayer is a "steering wheel." When faced with an important decision, believers seek God's direction. In Acts 13:1–3, the church in Antioch was praying and fasting when the Holy Spirit spoke through the prophets, instructing: "Set apart for me Barnabas and Saul for the work to which I have called them" (v. 3). Likewise, the psalmist celebrates: "The steps of a good man are ordered by the Lord: and he delighteth in his way" (Ps 37:23 KJV). God does not want us to stumble around in the darkness. He will guide us to the path that we should take.

Fasting, a Discipline of the Body

Fasting is going without food during a time of special prayer. It can be on a regular basis (such as every Wednesday or Friday) or sporadic. Kelli Mahoney observes that fasting is about "feeding the spirit through our obedience to God."[1] When the disciples came back from town and found Jesus speaking with the Samaritan woman at the well, they urged him to eat something. Jesus replied: "I have food to eat that you know nothing about" (John 4:32). Jesus later explained that his "food" was to "do the will of him who sent me and to finish his work" (4:34). Fasting is an acknowledgment that "man shall not live on bread alone, but on every word that comes from the mouth of God" (Matt 4:4). It is a reminder of what matters most, that the stomach and bodily appetites are not to rule over us. These are temporal and will not last (1 Cor 6:13), but the things of God have enduring value.

The Lord seems to have assumed that his followers would fast. In Matthew 6:16, he advised his disciples that "when you fast" they should not make a show of fasting. Rather, they were to abstain from food in a low-key way. If someone asks if you would like a piece of cake, a "no thank you" will suffice. Should they press the point, state quietly: "I'm fasting," then change the subject.

In Acts 13:1–3, the church added fasting to their prayers while seeking direction from God. During a fast, our spiritual senses become more keenly attuned. As we hunger for food, our prayer becomes: "Lord, let me be as hungry for you as I am hungry for food." During an extended fast, hunger pains will usually subside after the third day. Some experience no hunger pains at all. Often, those who fast will allow themselves occasional breath mints since halitosis is one of fasting's side-effects.

Fasting can be done in various ways. A partial fast is abstaining from certain rich foods for a time (Dan 1:8–16). Others will go from one day to two weeks without food but drinking ample amounts of water and (perhaps) taking a vitamin supplement.

The outer limit for how long the human body can go without food before beginning to metabolize its own muscle is forty days. Jesus fasted from food (but drank water) for forty days in the wilderness—see Matthew 4:1–11. The victory over the devil and the spiritual power that he gained from the fast propelled his ministry

---

1. Mahoney, "Biblical Verses on Fasting."

and is sometimes taken as a model by church leaders today who face spiritual opposition. A full fast is abstaining from both food and drink for up to seventy-two hours. Going longer than this without liquid may be life threatening. Before undertaking any fast, consult with your medical professional to be sure that you have no condition that would be aggravated by fasting.

Summing It All Up

When it comes to spiritual respiration, "breathing in" includes the disciplines of prayer and fasting. Prayer is talking to God and listening for God's voice. Likewise, fasting accompanies prayer for a season, hungering for God more than food, seeking divine direction or engaging in spiritual combat as Jesus did in the wilderness.

Prayer and fasting are disciplines of the spirit and body, respectively, yet there are also disciplines of the mind. Let us turn in the next chapter to Christian education, loving God with all of our mind.

Questions for Discussion

1. The author notes that prayer is both speaking to God and listening to God. When you pray, which do you find easier? Why?

2. Those who pray should not expect to hear an audible voice from the Lord. However, we can still know when God has spoken. How would you explain this distinction?

3. Jesus said: "*When* you fast"(Matt 6:16a). In your view, is fasting in the church today a common practice or neglected? If neglected, what time of the year would be an appropriate time for believers to fast together?

4. Does fasting obligate God to answer our prayers? If not, what is the purpose of fasting?

8

Christian Education: Digging Deeper, Building Higher

I LOVE SKYSCRAPERS. IF visiting a new city, I'll often head straight for the tallest building and—as long as the fee isn't too much—take the elevator to the observation deck. There's nothing like the view you can get of the city when perched up so high!

I've learned a few things about how engineers design skyscrapers. The more floors tall a building is, the deeper the foundation must be. That's a good picture of how the church should think about education. The church encourages education of all kinds for her people because she knows that God is not glorified by ignorance. Jesus never saw a contradiction between heart and head. He called us to love God with all of our heart, soul, strength *and* mind (Matt 22:37). Jesus invites us: "Build high!" Followers of Christ are free to pursue truth and discovery in all its forms, but to build higher, we must first dig deeper.

Digging Deeper

The psalmist affirms: "The fear of the LORD is the beginning of wisdom. All who practice it have a good understanding" (Ps 111:10a ESV). God is the sure foundation upon which we can build in all areas of life, including educationally. Saint Augustine (d. 430 AD) called this "faith seeking understanding."

The Jewish people knew how important it was to properly teach their children about God. In Deuteronomy 6:6–8, God commands:

> These commandments that I give you today are to be on your hearts. Impress them on your children. Talk about them when you sit at home and when you walk along the road, when you lie down and when you get up. Tie them as symbols on your hands and bind them on your foreheads. Write them on the doorframes of your houses and on your gates.

Children are like wet cement. It is never a question of *whether* they will be imprinted but only *who* will do the imprinting.

Parents are a child's first teachers, and when it comes to learning about God, they turn to us. Once when our older son was only three years old, he was thinking about the song that he had learned in Sunday School, "He's got the whole world in his hands." As we drove in the car, his question was earnest: "Mom and Dad, does God really have the whole world in his hands?" "Yes," I replied, "God really does." There was a long pause. Finally, he replied: "God must have *really* big hands!"

Theologians can debate the finer points of whether God as spirit can have hands (John 4:34). To do so is to miss the point. The imagery of "big hands" is a lesson about God's immensity, that God is bigger than creation—and, by extension—bigger than any problem we face.

Not all lessons about God taught by parents are helpful. A mother warned her son: "Even if I can't see what you're doing, God sees." While this may be true, is it helpful? She planted in the young mind of her son an image not of God as a loving Father who forgives and can help us rise above our failures, but rather a divine version of the CCTV monitoring cameras used by countries to track their own citizens. We must be careful what we teach and how we teach it, nurturing in our children a desire to draw near to God as one who is not only bigger than our problems but also loving, gracious, and worthy of our trust.

One program that helps build deep faith foundations is Bible quizzing. The Bible itself encourages memorization of Scripture (Ps 119:11) and few programs have been as successful in grounding youth in God's written Word. In moments of uncertainty, passages memorized serve as an internal moral compass, guiding us to make decisions that are pleasing to God.

Yet Christian education—at home or at church—should focus not just on Bible memorization but also discovering how each of us fits into what Michael Lodahl calls the "Story of God." That story in the sixty-six books of the Old and New Testaments reveals God as a tri-unity (Trinity), God the Father, God the Son, and God the Holy Spirit. Knowing that some of the subjects they would discuss could be unsettling, a theology professor was wise. He would always begin his class by inviting students to recite the Apostles' Creed, the foundational, ancient summary of that story of faith:

> I believe in God, the Father Almighty, Creator of heaven and earth; and in Jesus Christ, His only Son, our Lord: Who was conceived by the Holy Spirit, born of the Virgin Mary; suffered under Pontius Pilate, was crucified, died and was buried. He descended to the dead; the third day He rose again from the dead; He ascended into heaven, is seated at the right hand of God the Father Almighty; from thence He shall come to judge the living and the dead. I believe in the Holy Spirit, the Holy Catholic Church, the communion of Saints, the forgiveness of sins, the resurrection of the body, and life everlasting. Amen.

Educating our children in the things of God begins at the youngest age. It is the task of parents and other members of the household of faith to bring them up to love God. While learning about God is lifelong, many churches make a point to catechize children around the age of twelve. Catechism is a system of questions and responses that a child memorizes. Some traditions call this "foundations of faith." It is another opportunity to make sure that our children have experienced the transformational grace of Christ in their lives, that for them Jesus is not just the Savior of

Part One: Breathing In

the world but their Savior. Children who have not yet decided to follow Jesus can be encouraged to make that decision.

Easter Sunday is traditionally the day when new believers are baptized. Graduates from the catechism class who have a clear profession of Christian faith but who have not yet been baptized should be given the opportunity to be baptized by immersion, pouring, or sprinkling. Since Christian baptism is a sacrament of initiation and therefore is not repeatable (Eph 4:5), those who at the request of their parents were already baptized as infants or young children can publicly participate in a ritual that reaffirms what their parents did for them.

Building Higher

Because God calls us to love the Lord with all of our mind, the people of God are not threatened by education in all its forms. Rather, they embrace it as another expression of their worship. Though the emperor Charlemagne (d. 814 AD) was wrong to not allow for the education of girls, he is to be commended for requiring cathedrals and monasteries to provide a course of study for intelligent boys who also had the desire to learn. Later, Pope Gregory VII (1073–85) insisted that clergy be well educated, leading over time to the founding in the mid-twelfth century of the first university (the famed "Sorbonne") attached to the Cathedral of Notre Dame in Paris. Areas of study included theology, philosophy, law, mathematics, and medicine. Such openness to both the book of revelation (Scripture) and nature's book (science) was the seedbed that would later produce men like Gregor Mendel (1822–84), an Austrian monk who became a renowned geneticist.

Besides Roman Catholicism, the Reformed tradition of Christianity (birthed in the early sixteenth century) has taught that "all truth is God's truth." Celebrated English physicist Isaac Newton (b. 1642) was also a man of abiding faith, writing extensively in the fields of science and theology. This dual curiosity was shared by the Anglican priest and cofounder of Methodism, John Wesley (1703–91). Wesley was fascinated by medicine, and wrote a book outlining remedies for common ailments. He also developed a machine used to shock those suffering from depression, a crude precursor to twentieth-century electroshock therapy.

Today, this ability to see science and Christian faith as compatible—not contradictory—lives on in persons like John Polkinghorne, an accomplished theoretical physicist who later became an Anglican priest. His attitude reflects the maxim of Bertha Munro, the late longtime dean of Eastern Nazarene College: "There is no conflict between the best of education and the best in the Christian religion."

Far from undermining Christian faith, encouraging our children to pursue knowledge in whatever academic discipline they choose will often establish their faith. It gives them the confident message that our faith is robust, not like a fragile teacup, ready to shatter under the slightest pressure. Psalm 19:1 celebrates: "The heavens declare the glory of God; the skies proclaim the work of his hands." Because God is the Creator, the creation will point to its author, like a painting tells us something of the character of the painter.

Summing It All Up

Christian education is like a skyscraper. With Christian faith as a solid foundation, we invite our people to build the skyscraper of knowledge higher than ever before. Yet to build higher, we must first dig deeper. For the people of God, education is founded upon the fear of the Lord, then builds upward. The pursuit of knowledge in all its forms is not an affront to God but a noble expression of what it means to love God with all of our mind. This is our duty, and this is our joy.

Knowledge of God gained through Christian education becomes practical when applied in a life accountable to other believers. No practice across history has proven as fruitful for taking believers to the next level of their faith journey than meeting together in small groups. It is this vital aspect of discipleship that we will examine in the next chapter.

PART ONE: BREATHING IN

Questions for Discussion

1. Have you ever participated in catechism or Bible memorization? If so, share your experience with the group. How did it impact your spiritual development?

2. Read the Apostles' Creed together in unison. What phrases are striking to you? Why?

3. What does the expression "all truth is God's truth" mean? Do you agree that Christians are free to pursue knowledge wherever it leads without fear of it threatening their faith? Why or why not?

9

Independence or Interdependence? The Power of Small Groups

WE EXPECTED TO RUN alone. That's how our former cross-country coach did it. But on his first day, our new coach explained then demonstrated a different way of running together. He called it "Indian running." Coach laced on his running shoes and ordered: "Follow me."

Quickly we formed a line, like baby chicks following their mother hen. Setting a brisk pace, after a minute, coach barked out his command: "Next runner." The boy at the back of the line then sprinted, passing his teammates, taking his position at the front of the line as the new leader. After another minute, he, too, would shout: "Next runner" and a new leader emerged. In this way, everyone had a chance to set the pace for a time. No longer were we nine runners depending only upon ourselves. Instead, we were interdependent, encouraging each other, running together. Coach taught us all an important lesson: *Interdependence beats independence every time.*

The wisdom literature of the Old Testament teaches the power of interdependence. Ecclesiastes 4:9–12 explains:

> Two are better than one,
> > because they have a good return for their labor:
> If either of them falls down,
> > one can help the other up.
> But pity anyone who falls
> > and has no one to help them up.

Part One: Breathing In

> Also, if two lie down together, they will keep warm.
> But how can one keep warm alone?
> Though one may be overpowered,
> two can defend themselves.
> A cord of three strands is not quickly broken.

Likewise, Paul encouraged the Galatians to carry each other's burdens as a way of fulfilling Christ's law of love (Gal 6:2). In the earliest days of the church in Jerusalem, this was how believers built each other up in the faith, sharing their possessions, meeting in each other's homes, eating together, celebrating Holy Communion, praying and encouraging one another (Acts 2:42–47). It was an attractive, loving fellowship, and outsiders longed to be part of it.

What worked in the earliest centuries still worked hundreds of years later. The young English evangelist John Wesley (1703–91), was instrumental in birthing many people into Christian faith. However, he noticed that their faith often quickly grew cold. Like a newborn baby needs a blanket to keep warm, so new believers need warm fellowship to grow in their faith. Wesley soon despaired of visiting in the homes of everyone who was coming to Christ. He had to find a new system. Over time, he organized the early Methodists into mixed male/female groups of fifteen to twenty ("classes") and—for those who desired—into single gender "bands" of five to seven. These small groups met once per week in the evening for sixty to ninety minutes, allowing people to share their successes and challenges with each other, to pray and encourage each other in their faith. Like the early Christians, the Methodists discovered that—while independence leads to spiritual indifference—interdependence fosters spiritual growth.

Small groups are discipleship groups, helping members follow Jesus more closely, together. Paradoxically, greater dependence upon each other leads to greater dependence upon God.

While serving as a missionary in Benin (West Africa), I always looked forward to the Wednesday morning men's breakfast. Five or six of the male missionaries in town met each week at 7 a.m. at the same café. We drank coffee, ate eggs and toast, caught up on events from the last week, and encouraged each other. Before leaving, we spent ten or fifteen minutes in prayer. Those were years of great challenge in ministry, and our weekly meetings were fresh water for my thirsty spirit. Though we never ran together, those Wednesday breakfasts reminded me of Indian runs from high school. Once again, I moved from independence to interdependence, growing stronger in the process.

In small groups, we learn that our struggles are not ours alone. With time, trust develops between members. Brothers and sisters feel free to share about unhealthy habits that have ensnared them and receive help from others in the group. In the confession of sin and praying for each other, healing comes (Jas 5:16).

To be independent leads to isolation and despair. Interdependence, on the other hand, builds community and together draws us closer to God. What small group opportunities are there in your church? If there are none, speak with your pastor or other leaders in your church. Reflect how you can become a catalyst to begin this powerful initiative in your community of faith.

Questions for Discussion

1. Think of a small circle of which you've been part in the past, whether a club or service organization. What was it about the group that kept you coming back?
2. Discuss the difference between "independence" and "interdependence." What are the advantages and pitfalls of both?
3. Is it possible to be fully dependent upon God yet also interdependent toward others? If so, how do these two concepts relate to each other?

Part Two

Breathing Out

10

God's Not-So-Secret Plan to Save Creation

IT'S A CLASSIC SCENE in television's *West Wing*. Josh Lyman mistakenly announces to the White House press corps that the president has a "secret plan to fight inflation." His colleagues rib him mercilessly.

As it turns out, God is nothing like Mr. Lyman. The divine plan is not to fight inflation but to save creation, and it's not at all a secret. In fact, Jesus announces it openly: "For this is how God loved the world: He gave his one and only Son, so that everyone who believes in him will not perish but have eternal life" (John 3:16 NLT).

The Greek word translated as "world" is *cosmos*. It can also be translated as "universe." God—the creator of the universe—has a deep and abiding love for all creation. Psalm 145:9 affirms: "The LORD is good to all, and his mercy is over all that he has made" (ESV). Later, Psalm 149 calls on all creation to praise the LORD. Nothing is excluded—sun, moon, stars, angels, human beings, the creatures of the ocean depths, animals that scurry along the ground—all must give glory to the creator. In Isaiah's vision, even trees join the people of God in joyful song (Isa 55:12).

The Catastrophe

Yet something has gone terribly wrong in creation. Something is broken and must be repaired. Paul explained the devastating

PART TWO: BREATHING OUT

consequences of our first parents' poor choice to disobey God. Death was the result of sin, or disobedience (Rom 5:12). This disastrous consequence rippled out to damage all that God had perfectly made. Romans 8:20–21 tells us: "Against its will, all creation was subjected to God's curse. But with eager hope, the creation looks forward to the day when it will join God's children in glorious freedom from death and decay."

In the first section of *Mere Ecclesiology*, we looked at the people of God (the church) and the "breathing in" of practices that form God's people into Christ's image. Beginning in this chapter, we focus on the church's mission, her "breathing out" in service to the world. *What are the people of God supposed to do?* God wants to use us as partners to repair what is broken: God's intent is transformation, to restore to its original state all that God has made. It's a not-so-secret plan to save creation. And what is the catalyst that God will use to do that? It's you, it's me, and it's us as the church, a monumental mission inspired by our immense God. Yet too often in the past, our mission has been truncated, as if God cared only about the spiritual condition of individuals. In fact, God wants to make us disciples not as an end in itself, but as a means to a far broader end. This is the transformational mission of the people of God, to be God's instruments of change in our families, our community, our culture, and nature itself, redeeming the very biological ecosystem that sustains us. (We'll look at this theme more in chapter 14, our Christian commitment to ecology).

The Kingdom

In the Gospel of Matthew, God's not-so-secret plan to save creation is described using the language of "kingdom." Sometimes Jesus speaks of the "kingdom of God" (see Matt 13). Other times, he speaks of the "kingdom of heaven" (5:19–20; 7:21). Whichever term is used, it is clear that the kingdom is the solution to what has gone awry in creation, due to humanity's sin. Jesus taught his disciples to pray: "Your kingdom come, your will be done on earth, as it is in heaven" (Matt 6:10). The church and the kingdom are not synonymous; rather, the church is the instrument—empowered by the Holy Spirit—through which Christ establishes his kingdom.

Rock, Ripples, and Results

If we could only have one gospel, I would choose Luke. It's an amazing story of the difference Jesus of Nazareth makes in our world. The birth narrative in Luke 1–2 announces the coming of the Son of God to earth, the incarnation, the divine clothing itself in human flesh.

Have you ever dropped a rock into a pond? What happens? The rock makes ripples. In a way, Jesus is like a rock that God the Father dropped into the pond of human existence. If Luke gives us the story of the rock, Jesus of Nazareth, then Acts is about the ripples and the results. In Acts 1:8, Jesus tells his eleven disciples that they must wait for the power of the Holy Spirit, who would live inside of them. Then—and only then—could they effectively ripple out, impacting others in positive, life-changing ways: "But you will receive power when the Holy Spirit has come upon you, and you will be my witnesses in Jerusalem and in all Judea and Samaria, and to the end of the earth" (Acts 1:8 ESV).

The Greek word for "power" is *dunamis*. It is the root from which we derive the English word "dynamite." When filled with the Holy Spirit, our lives ripple in powerful ways, positively influencing those around us. We become evidence of the transforming capability of the gospel.

Yet our world is highly change resistant. The forces of the status quo do not give in easily. Jesus found that out firsthand when they arrested, whipped, stripped, and hung him on a cross to die. Now on a hill outside Jerusalem, the resurrected Christ warns his disciples: "You will be my witnesses." The Greek word used in Acts 1:8 for "witnesses" is *marthures*, giving us our English word "martyr." This is no ordinary testimony they will bear, but a testimony even unto death. Among those who heard Jesus that day was Peter, who tradition tells us was himself crucified upside down, when he considered himself unworthy to die in the same manner as had

PART TWO: BREATHING OUT

Jesus. Likewise, Stephen became the first martyr, stoned to death for his Christian confession (Acts 7). Advance always comes at a cost. The early history of the church is a bloody one. Writing in the second century AD, Tertullian observed: "The blood of the martyrs is the seed of the church." What was true then is true today as numerous Christians in the Middle East are being martyred for no other offense than their faith in Christ.

Thankfully, the rock and the ripples are followed by *results*. Luke's account in Acts shows the Christian faith moving out in ever-wider circles. Individuals are transformed, leading to transformation of families, communities, and their pagan practices: Saul, Apollos, Lydia, Priscilla and Aquila, Cornelius and many more become testimonies of the explosive, transformational power of belief in the risen Lord.

Summing It All Up

God cares deeply about all creation, from human beings, communities, trees, and animals to the whole of creation, all of which were originally meant to praise the creator. Yet human sin—willful disobedience to God—marred what God had made perfect. Not willing to give up on what he had made, God in Christ has launched a not-so-secret plan to save creation. God's holy people, the church, are partners in that holy, transformational mission, a mission to extend God's kingdom. In the next chapter, we'll look at the ministry of healing and deliverance and the place that they play within the church as we cooperate with the Holy Spirit for the establishment of God's kingdom.

Questions for Discussion

1. The sin of our first parents, Adam and Eve, is often called "original sin" or "the fall," what the author calls "the catastrophe." Most Christian theologians teach that human beings by default are not good but evil until they yield themselves to the

grace of God. In what ways do your own observations in life affirm or challenge this idea?

2. The Greek word *cosmos* in John 3:16 can be translated as "world" or "universe." Should astronomers discover intelligent life on another planet, how might this affect how we think about God's desire to be in relationship with all that God has created?

3. Tertullian insisted: "The blood of the martyrs is the seed of the church." In what way does our firm Christian belief in the resurrection give us hope?

11

Healing and Deliverance

"HELLO—HAVE YOU BEEN WAITING *for me?*" As a boy, I remember this opening line from the radio program featuring American evangelist and faith healer Kathyrn Kuhlman (1907–76). I don't remember much of what she said to her radio audience, but her strange, undulating, and hypnotic voice did influence me all the same. I determined that anything having to do with healing must be really weird.

It's too bad that the odd ducks have scared us away from searching out a more biblical, balanced view when it comes to the topic of healing and deliverance. Such a study will show that these two emphases form part of the "breathing out" of the church, manifestations of the powerful movement of God's Holy Spirit in the world.

God's View of Embodied People: "Very Good"

The best place to begin a study of healing and deliverance is to go back to God's nature and how we are created. John tells us something profound about the divine character: "Whoever does not love does not know God, because God is love" (1 John 4:8). How did this God—whose very essence is love—make us? He could have made us as spirits, phantoms with no substance, yet God chose to make us *embodied* beings. We have legs and arms, feet and hands, hearts and brains. Scripture tells us that when God fashioned Adam out of the dust, he breathed into him the breath of life. And so Adam became a "living being" (Gen 2:7). Throughout

Healing and Deliverance

Genesis 1, God had declared his creation "good," but only when God had made the first human being did God pronounce creation "very good" (Gen 1:27). It's an excellent thing to be created by God and to be created with a body!

This stands in stark contrast with ideas developed by the Gnostics in the early centuries of Christianity. They believed that all matter—including human bodies—is corrupt and evil. The body was considered by them—and by some Greek philosophers before them—to be a prison for the soul. "Salvation" comes when pure spirits can be released from evil bodies.

Some modern Christians seem to have imbibed gnostic ideas. Instead of presenting the gospel in a holistic way, God's desire to renew all things, they focus only upon "winning souls." In their thinking, "getting saved" is synonymous with preparing disembodied souls for heaven. There is little concern for people's bodies; that's not the part that lasts, in their view. To the homeless, they might dish out a bowl of soup from time to time, but only as a means to reach the real objective, saving their souls.

You cannot have read this far in *Mere Ecclesiology* without knowing that inviting individuals to follow Jesus is a crucial part of what it means to be the church. There is no denying that God desperately wants to be in eternal fellowship with those whom he has created, and—because of what Jesus has done on the cross on our behalf—for them to be reconciled to God both now and forever (John 3:16; Eph 2:8–9). The problem arises when we so prioritize the "soul" that we dismiss the body as unimportant. Good Christians can disagree about whether human beings consist of body and soul (dualism) or just bodies animated by God's breath (holism/monism). Wherever one comes down on that philosophical issue, we must be careful not to consider people's bodily well being unimportant. We must not deem what God calls "very good" to be evil and therefore unworthy of our concern.

Part Two: Breathing Out

Jesus, Healer and Deliverer

God's concern to heal bodies and deliver people from all that oppresses them comes across most clearly in the ministry of Jesus of Nazareth. To inaugurate his ministry, Jesus in Luke 4:18 quoted the words of Isaiah 61:

> The Spirit of the Lord is on me,
> because he has anointed me
> to proclaim good news to the poor.
> He has sent me to proclaim freedom for the prisoners
> and recovery of sight for the blind,
> to set the oppressed free,
> to proclaim the year of the Lord's favor.

Mashangu Maluleka sees in this passage the threefold work of the church: preaching, healing, and deliverance, or PHD.[1] The four gospels are replete with stories of how Jesus ministered holistically, addressing both spiritual and physical needs. His was a ministry to the whole person; he fed the hungry, restored the sick to wellness and—where the devil oppressed individuals—confronted them and put them to flight. Having just raised Lazarus to life in John 11, it is astounding to hear these words from Jesus to his disciples just a few chapters later: "Very truly I tell you, whoever believes in me will do the works I have been doing, and they will do even greater things than these, because I am going to the Father" (John 14:12). The pattern given by Jesus was meant to continue.

Healing and Deliverance in the Early Church

In Acts 1, Jesus ascends to the Father. Acts 2 recounts the descent of the dove, the Holy Spirit falling on the 120 in the Upper Room in Jerusalem. This "breathing in" by the church of the Third Person of the Trinity soon results in a "breathing out" that takes the world by storm. Not only is Peter empowered to preach an

---

1. Crofford and Maluleka, "Let Them Call," 5.

anointed sermon (Acts 2:14–41), but he and John heal a lame man at the temple gate (Acts 3:1–10). God's healing power continues through Peter as people brought their sick and laid them on the path so that Peter's shadow could fall on them as he passed by, resulting in their healing (Acts 5:15). The very next verse continues: "Crowds gathered also from the towns around Jerusalem, bringing their sick and those tormented by impure spirits, and all of them were healed "(Acts 5:16). Another notable instance of deliverance from unclean spirits occurred when Paul cast out a fortune-telling demon from a slave girl (Acts 16:16–18). In these instances and more, the PHD pattern—preaching, healing, and deliverance—is clear throughout this second book written by Luke the physician, a sequel to his gospel and extraordinary in its account of the power of the Holy Spirit. Whereas the Holy Spirit in Luke's gospel was evidenced through the ministry of Jesus, in the book of Acts, it is manifest through the ministry of the church and her leaders. What Paul calls the "gifts of the Spirit" (1 Cor 12:1–11) were on full display, include the "gifts of healings" (Greek plural in 1 Cor 12:9) poured upon and channeled through the people of God. Likewise, James 5:3–16 is a snapshot of local congregations of believers who prayed for and anointed with oil those who were sick, trusting God for healing.

God's Healing through Medical Science and Natural Means

The late nineteenth-century teacher A. B. Simpson discouraged his followers from consulting with doctors.[2] However, most churches today recognize that God uses medical professionals as instruments of divine healing. Ben Carson, a pediatric neurosurgeon, is an example of a man of Christian faith whom God has used in amazing ways, including the first-ever separation of Siamese twins joined at the head. When serving as a missionary in West Africa, I was very grateful for the French physician who treated me with

---

2. Simpson, *Gospel of Healing*, 317–18.

Part Two: Breathing Out

anti-malarial medications when I came down with a severe case of malaria. Without her healing arts, I would not be here to write this book.

In the same way that pharmaceutical companies have researched remedies to numerous conditions, in many parts of Africa, herbal remedies have been passed on from one generation to the next. Fawzi Mahomoodally of the Department of Health Science of the University of Mauritius notes: "In many parts of rural Africa, traditional healers prescribing medicinal plants are the most easily accessible and affordable health resource available to the local community and at times the only therapy that subsists."[3] Believers must be discerning, however, between those who prescribe strictly herbal remedies and others who tap magical, ancestral, or occult powers. The former are harmless and may very well be helpful; the latter will expose the individual to harmful demonic influences.

On Counterfeit and Real Bills

In late 1993, my family and I arrived in Abidjan, Côte d'Ivoire, to take up our first missionary assignment. To outfit our house, we visited a large home furnishings store downtown. Credit cards were not accepted, so we came with a stack of bills to pay for our purchases. One by one, the cashier held the bills under a special light. When she paused extra long over a particular bill, I started to get nervous. "Sir," she said, "this bill is counterfeit." Taken aback, I blurted out: "Call the police!" By now the manager had come over. He looked at the bill, then replied: "If I call the police, they'll arrest *you*." That day I was cheated out of money because an unscrupulous money changer had duped me.

No one likes being duped. Because that experience left a bad taste in my mouth, I could have said: "I'll never use any money ever again!" But that would have been an overreaction. After all, *most* bills are genuine, even if *some* are counterfeit.

---

3. Mahomoodally, "Traditional Medicines in Africa."

Healing and Deliverance

In the area of healing, there are plenty of counterfeit bills circulating. There is counterfeit doctrine, claiming that our healing depends only upon having "enough faith," as if that were the only factor in play. Likewise, there are counterfeit practices. Robert Evans chronicles six "tricks" that he learned as a "faith healer," including hiring a hobo as an actor. For the finale, the homeless man hobbled up to the front with a cane, pretending to be lame so that he could be "healed."[4] In 2014, a Kenyan investigative news program, "Inside Story," debunked the "healing" practices of Victor Kanyari, who was shown to use elaborate playacting and false testimonies by collaborators. This journalistic exposé led to a government crackdown on the registration of new churches, damaging the trust that people placed in Christian leaders.[5]

In the face of counterfeit doctrine and practice surrounding healing, shall the church abandon it altogether? To do so would be throwing out the good bills with the fake ones. The church would be poorer for it, neglecting Christ's model of holistic ministry, involving preaching, healing, and deliverance (PHD). Is there a model for divine healing that is tied to the local congregation as outlined in James 5, thereby providing for accountability and minimizing the chance for unknown outside "healers" to dupe the people of God? Let us journey to Durban, South Africa, and look at how God is healing and delivering in the name of Jesus.

Jesus Heals a Brain Tumor

Pastor Gabriel Benjiman shepherds a congregation located in a Durban neighborhood that is predominantly Muslim but also with a Hindu population nearby. One Wednesday night while Gabriel was preaching, a fifteen-year-old Hindu girl, Risha (not her name), arrived with her mother, Sarah (not her name), and other family members. Following the sermon, they approached the pastor. "My daughter has not slept in weeks, she's unable to eat, and

---

4. Evans, "6 Tricks."
5. Zirulnick, "Kenya 'Miracle Worker' Scandal."

the doctors say she has a brain tumor," Sarah reported. Gabriel and others gathered around Risha and laid their hands on her. "I can't describe the sensation," Gabriel recalls. "It's almost as if my hands stiffened and there was an extreme heat." Risha turned and looked at Gabriel and started smiling, then laughing. She testified that she had no more pain in her head.

Pastor Gabriel urged the family to return to the doctor and have Risha scanned again. They discovered that the five-centimeter tumor on her left frontal lobe had diminished to half a centimeter. Gabriel was thrilled, but cautioned: "The Lord who began this good work will not leave it incomplete. We need to pray and ask the Lord to complete it." So he and the church leaders gathered around again, laid hands on Risha and prayed. A subsequent scan showed that the tumor was gone! The doctor even called in another physician to confirm his opinion. The tumor has not returned nor has the pain.

Jesus Delivers from a Demon

Pastor Titus Joseph leads a congregation outside Durban. After nearly resigning because the church was not growing, Titus spent three days on a nearby mountain, praying and fasting. Since his return to the church, Jesus has used him as an instrument in a number of healings and deliverances, divine miracles that Titus attributes to the congregation's dedication to prayer and fasting. The church is growing, there is excitement among the people, and God is at work.

While some deny the existence of demons, Pastor Titus knows from his own firsthand experience that demons exist, but that Jesus also delivers. In 2011, sixteen-year-old Jacob (not his name) had dabbled in Satanic worship. A family member brought him to the church. He couldn't go to school, he couldn't sleep, he couldn't eat. Pastor Titus recounts: "The devil wanted to take his life away. This young boy, under the influence of a demon, drank brake fluid. His family brought him to church, and the demon said: 'He's going to die. He drank brake fluid.'" At the hospital, they saved his life, but the next day he was at home, still demon possessed. Jacob became violent, so his family called Pastor Titus and other church leaders to the house. When Jacob was in the bathroom, his bed caught spontaneously on fire, a demonic manifestation. They put him in the next room, and started to pray for him. Eventually, the demons left when the pastor and his team identified each of them by name and cast them out in the name of Jesus.

An Empty House, Swept Clean

When it comes to deliverance from demons, Jesus cautioned that a spiritual vacuum must not be left in the heart of the person who is delivered:

> When an impure spirit comes out of a person, it goes through arid places seeking rest and does not find it. Then it says, "I will return to the house I left." When it arrives, it finds the house swept clean and put in order. Then it goes and takes seven other spirits more wicked than itself, and they go in and live there. And the final condition of that person is worse than the first. (Luke 10:24–26)

Pastors Benjiman and Joseph recounted numerous stories of healing and deliverance beyond the two told in this chapter. In each case, the person healed and delivered was lovingly folded into the life of the church. Individually, they made decisions to follow Christ and began growing in their faith. In the same way, churches that desire to be used of God in PHD ministry must provide intentional discipleship, coming alongside new brothers and sisters in the faith, encircling them and protecting them from further diabolical attack.

When God Chooses Not to Heal

While we obey the Lord and pray for the sick, rejoicing in the healing and deliverance God gives, experience tells us that sometimes God does not heal. As a pastor, I called our church leaders forward and we laid our hands on Edna. Though she had received radiation treatment, her cancer was advanced and her prognosis grim. We anointed her with oil and prayed for her healing. Less than two months later, Edna passed away. On another occasion in a single worship service, I heard both testimonies to God's miraculous healing and requests for prayer for those grieving the loss of a loved one, someone for whom they had spent anguished hours praying for healing. If God always healed when we pray, there would be human beings walking around on earth who are hundreds, even thousands of years old. The Bible reminds us that there is a time to be born and a time to die (Eccl 3:2). As Christians, we do not believe that death has the last word. Like the Apostles' Creed affirms, we believe in the resurrection of the body and the life everlasting! Any teaching on healing is incomplete without that important and forward-looking affirmation of faith.

Summing It All Up

The Holy Spirit empowers the church in many ways. These include preaching, healing, and deliverance. While counterfeits exist, this should not deter God's people, the church, from "breathing out" and pouring the oil of God's healing into a sin-sick world. As we do, people will be drawn to the holistic message that God cares for human beings both spiritually and physically.

While God may not use every follower of Christ to bring physical healing and deliverance, the Lord has a calling for each of us. It is to this topic that we turn in the next chapter.

Questions for Discussion

1. The author maintains that God's love for us includes his care and concern for our bodies. Why is this an important understanding when it comes to the doctrine and practice of healing and deliverance?

2. Discuss Mashangu Maluleka's insistence that the ministry of the church must be all about PHD—preaching, healing, and deliverance. Which of these seems to be the strongest in the church where you attend? How can the other elements be strengthened?

3. In what ways can the synergism between the healing arts of medical professionals and church-led prayers for healing and deliverance be strengthened?

4. C. S. Lewis in the preface to his *Screwtape Letters* warned against two extremes regarding the devil and demons, namely, "disbelieving in their existence" or feeling "an excessive and unhealthy interest in them." What consequences might there be for a church that falls into either extreme?

12

Discover Your Calling

A SIXTY-SOMETHING EXECUTIVE LAMENTED: "I spent my life climbing the ladder of success, only to discover that my ladder was leaning against the wrong wall." How many can identify with his sad observation?

Money earned, luxurious houses owned, or fancy cars acquired are often the measures of success in our world. Yet some swim against the stream, enjoying the content that comes not from acquiring but from calling. The late missionary Ron Farris gave up a very comfortable salary as a surgeon in the Midwestern United States, relocating with his family to tropical West Africa. After eight years of missionary service in a church-sponsored urban clinic treating tropical diseases, he lost his life when hijackers took control of the jet he was on, crashing it into the ocean off Africa's southeast coast. Later, a missionary colleague attended his funeral back in the United States. Behind her sat some of Dr. Farris's former surgical colleagues from the United States. They lamented that his life had been "wasted." During the funeral service, however, many spoke of the impact Ron had made in West Africa, including the treatment of more than thirty thousand patients annually, poor people who had nowhere else to go. Following the funeral, the same medical colleagues who had been so critical revised their assessment, admitting: "Maybe his life wasn't such a waste after all."

If income is the only measure of success, then some of history's best-known personalities were utter failures. Mother Teresa labored among the destitute of Calcutta, never having much to show for it. Likewise, Rev. Martin Luther King Jr. never had a large bank account, but his riches lay elsewhere. He received the gratitude of African Americans who followed him into a new era of civil rights in a country that too often turned a blind eye to racial abuses. Nelson Mandela, for his part, spent twenty-seven years of his life without income, locked up in state-run prisons. Yet "Madiba" led South Africa from the dark days of apartheid into a place where racial reconciliation could begin.

What Is Your Calling?

In each of these four instances, individuals found their niche. In Christian terms, the niche God has reserved for followers of Jesus Christ is one's calling. Every believer has a *general* calling, to live a righteous life that is pleasing to God (1 Pet 1:16; Rom 12:1–2). However, the testimony of Scripture is that God also has a *specific* calling for each of us to fulfill. Some callings are more dramatic, such as John the Baptist's calling to "prepare the way" for the Messiah (Isa 40:3; Matt 3:3) or Saul's Damascus road experience where Jesus sent him as a light to the Gentiles (Acts 26:17). Other callings are simpler but no less valid, such as Dorcas's quilt making (Acts 9:36–43).

A synonym of calling is "vocation." Vocation is found at the nexus between our God-given abilities and an urgent problem that cries out for a solution. Both vocation and calling move us beyond merely identifying something that we *can* do in life to what we *must* do, no matter how difficult. Christian experience teaches us that we will have a lingering sense of discontent and unease when we are on the wrong track. On the other hand, when we are correctly responding to the Holy Spirit's direction, an unwavering peace will be ours.

Everyone a Minister: Ephesians 4:11–13

In the past, the church made a serious error in the way it spoke of "the minister." It reserved this term for individuals who sought ordination by the church. Thankfully, we are recovering a more biblical understanding of ministry as taught in passages like Ephesians 4:11–13. There, Paul teaches that there are five categories of those who equip believers for ministry. These are the apostles, prophets, evangelists, pastors, and teachers. What is their task? They are to equip all of God's people for "works of service" (4:12). The result is that the body of Christ is "built up" and "mature" (v. 13a). Only then can the church attain the "whole measure of the fullness of Christ" (v. 13b).

A local church I visited understood Paul's teaching well. On the front of their worship folder, it gave the name of the pastor. Underneath, it listed "ministers" as "the whole congregation." All of us have a service to perform in the world, a calling from God. For some, this will mean ordination in the church, but for most, our divine calling will be in other areas, whether business, medicine, law, teaching, or a dozen other pursuits. In some cases, calling does not exclude the accumulation of wealth, but for such a believer, he or she has an even greater responsibility to wisely steward God's resources (Luke 12:48b; Matt 10:8). For many, however, calling will not intersect with material riches. Yet being where God wants us to be is its own reward, and our place of contented service will be the area where God can best use our gifts for maximum impact to build the kingdom.

Tony Flores, Urban Music Teacher

Tony Flores is an example of a Christ follower who has found his calling in the classroom.[1] With family roots in Monterey, Mexico, Tony spent most of his growing up years in Galena Park, Texas, the adopted son of a pastor's family. Galena Park was not an easy atmosphere. Of all US cities, its adults ranked as the seventy-fifth worst educated, with only 50 percent having completed high school and a mere 7 percent earning a college degree. Despite these obstacles, Tony was inspired by some of his teachers who believed in him and spurred him on in his primary and secondary school studies.

---

1. Quotes and anecdotes throughout this section are taken from an interview with the author, April 14, 2016.

He eventually graduated with his music education degree from a Christian university in Oklahoma City.

Mr. Flores—as his students call him—now teaches K–5 general music, choir, and ballroom dance at Wiley Post Elementary, a Title 1 school located in an economically challenged sector of Oklahoma City.

As a "preacher's kid," Tony thought that ministry had to be in the church. But as he began teaching at Wiley Post, his thinking changed: "Ministry doesn't need to happen in front of a pulpit," he reflected. "I realized that I can be Christ and show the love of God at my job. God's work can be done in so many different ways." He came to this realization one November. Tony had distributed special shirts to choir members to wear for the Veteran's Day concert. Everyone wore the shirt to the concert except Susan (name changed). After he took her aside before the concert, she explained that she hadn't been able to wash the shirt in time. "I have extra shirts," he said. Susan then began to cry. She explained that the day before, she and her dad had been together in the living room when someone came to the door, shot, and killed him. Despite that traumatic event, Susan insisted on coming to sing in the choir concert, explaining to her mother: "Mr. Flores expects me there." Tony didn't know what to say at the time, but looking back at the incident, concluded: "It was then that I realized that there is much work left to be done in this building, not to mention this community. From that point, I realized that this is a ministry/calling. This was a defining moment for me, and I knew that I was doing exactly what God wanted me to do."

When students seem unresponsive, Tony has learned that they're usually listening and eventually will do the right thing. "It's kind of like when God talks to us and we don't pay any attention, but finally do what he wants, " Tony suggests. Such was the case with Adam (name changed). He and his brothers were among the toughest cases he had seen in his fifth grade music class, coming from a highly dysfunctional home environment, but Tony never felt like more of a failure than the day he heard that Adam had been sent to juvenile hall. But when released, Adam took a new path. He began to get A's in his classes and his behavior stabilized. Later, he admitted to Mr. Flores: "That whole time I was in juvenile hall, I was upset because that isn't what you told me to do. You're the only person that has had my back." As a teacher in a public school, he is limited in how openly he can share his faith, but Tony is sanguine: "You can be Christlike without even mentioning him. People will see him in your actions."

In 2015, Mr. Flores was named Teacher of the Year at Wiley Post, then for the Putnam City School District. He was one of twelve finalists for Oklahoma Teacher of the Year, a follower of Christ living out his calling, making music and giving hope to children in what otherwise is too often a hopeless environment. "I can't reach every child," Tony admits, "but if I'm affecting one life, that's one life that the world just got better by. Everyone has the opportunity to affect one life."

Tammy Thomas, English Teacher in Rural Kansas

From Oklahoma City, just a few hours' drive northwest will take you to the farming communities of rural Kansas. It is in one of those small towns that Tammy Thomas has taught high school English, speech, and drama for the past fourteen years.[2] The setting in some ways is reminiscent of her own upbringing in a small town on the plains of Illinois, one of six children born to a loving and churchgoing family.

In their Kansas town, Tammy's husband, Bill, pastors one of the churches situated on the main road. "Since we live in a small town, people know me and they know my husband. They know he's a pastor," Tammy observes. "One of my favorite subjects to teach is British Literature. Literature lends itself to moral questions and it allows me to be open about my faith. I can legally answer any question a student asks me, even about God, but I don't give the Four Spiritual Laws in class, of course. Some of my students have been of others faith, such as Buddhist, Shinto, or Muslim."

2. Quotes and anecdotes throughout this section are taken from an interview with the author, April 14, 2016.

Tammy did not always view teaching as her calling. In fact, while living in Oklahoma, the Christian school attached to the church where Bill was pastoring needed a teacher, and the principal kept after her knowing that she had a degree in English. Tammy delayed for months, but finally agreed to give it a try. "But from the moment I started to teach that first day," she reflects, "it was like I had come home. I knew then that this was what God had formed me to do. It became this deep urgency in me to do it and to do it well, but also to be Christ in my classroom."

Her sense of calling has kept her through difficult times. At one of the schools where she has taught, an administrator—though a gifted person—didn't know how to get the best out of the teachers. Instead, his actions and attitude discouraged everyone, including the students. Tammy found it a challenge each day to get up and go to work. She prayed a lot during that time. At the height of her discouragement, one of her female colleagues advised: "Remember, Tammy, this is not about us. It's about the kids." It was just what Tammy needed to hear. Tammy concluded: "The kids still needed to know that I believed in them, and I needed to show them that this is how a Christian goes about work. And the Lord did it. He brought me through." That administrator eventually left the school and education altogether, but Tammy continued.

Along with challenges come joys. Elm (not his name) was a foreign exchange student in her British Literature course and was among her most conscientious students. It's the tradition during the graduation ceremony for students to give a rose to their parents. Occasionally, some students would buy an extra rose and give it to one of the teachers who had impacted their lives. Tammy had never received a rose, but that was about to change. "Mrs. Thomas," she heard someone say. She turned and there stood Elm with a rose in his hand. As he offered the rose, Tammy started to sob. Elm later returned to his home country, but Tammy still keeps in touch with him on social media. "I don't know if I made any spiritual impact on him," she confesses, "but he did on me—his kindness, his sensitivity. And every once in a while I'll pray for him, that he'll maybe remember something that I said. I pray that the right person will come along and will lead him to Christ."

Through both good times and bad, Tammy has kept things in perspective. "I really do believe that teaching is a calling from God. It has been for me." A verse that often comes to mind for her is Colossians 3:23: "Whatever you do, work at it wholeheartedly as though you were doing it for the Lord and not merely for people" (ISV). She concludes: "You have to approach everything that way. The way you do it should bring honor to God."

Summing It All Up

God has a general calling for every believer. It is the call to live a holy life, to please the Lord by our actions and words. But the Lord also has a specific calling for each of us, a place where we can best use the gifts that God has given to us. It is here that we can have maximum impact for the kingdom. Have you discovered your calling?

Responding to God's calling upon our lives is one way that followers of Christ can change the world. In the next chapter, we'll look at other ways God intends us to impact our community.

Questions for Discussion

1. Reread Ephesians 4:11–13. What is the task that God has given to the five types of leaders within the church?
2. What does the author mean when he says that "everyone is a minister"?
3. The chapter claims that "vocation" is found at "the nexus between our God-given abilities and an urgent problem that cries out for a solution." Do you agree? Why or why not?
4. Talk about the stories of Mr. Flores and Mrs. Thomas. How did having a sense that God called them to teach allow them to face difficult situations?

13

Impact Your Community

I'LL CALL THEM SUSAN and Lisa. Though their names have been changed, their story hasn't. Susan had since childhood been angry. She could lash out viciously toward others, but then something happened. Susan met Jesus and Jesus changed Susan. Sweetness replaced bitterness and church became a regular part of her life as she grew in her faith.

Her sister, Lisa, noticed. "What happened to you?" she asked Susan. "You used to be so angry." Susan told Lisa about her newfound faith in Christ. Lisa was intrigued and started going to church with Susan. Soon, Lisa also decided to follow Jesus.

When God transforms the lives of individuals, the impact ripples to others. In Acts 1, Jesus talks about this ever-widening impact. The Lord predicted the coming of the Holy Spirit and the change that would make in the lives of his followers. The disciples (followers) would become apostles (sent ones). Like a stone dropped in a pond, ripples would spread out in all directions: "But you will receive power when the Holy Spirit comes on you; and you will be my witnesses in Jerusalem, and in all Judea and Samaria, and to the ends of the earth" (Acts 1:8).

Jesus' words serve as a brief outline for the twenty-eight chapters of Acts. The transformation God desired began with the Jewish people on the Day of Pentecost, gathered in Jerusalem. Pilgrims who had gathered for the Jewish feast returned to their homes in other parts of the world, but some did not return the same as they came. They had believed in Jesus and their lives would never be the same; they took their new faith with them.

Part Two: Breathing Out

Later, a second wave rippled out from the epicenter as persecution drove many believers out of Jerusalem. They, too, would impact others wherever they went. Paul of Tarsus—who at first persecuted Christians—became one himself. With his traveling companions, they crossed over cultural and linguistic barriers becoming the first Christian missionaries. Wherever they went, the power of the gospel message transformed individuals, families, communities, and even the culture itself.

Families Transformed

But let's come back to that place in the pond where the stone first falls in. What does the first ring that ripples out represent? For Susan, that first ring—her Jerusalem—was her family. Her sister, Lisa, noticed the change in her life but didn't know why the change had taken place. By sharing her story with Lisa, her sister also came to faith.

John's gospel shows a similar effect. Jesus first called Andrew to follow him. The first thing he did was to find his brother, Simon, and tell him: "We have found the Messiah." John 1:42 records: "And he brought him to Jesus." Christian faith travels through family networks.

In the book of Acts, the term *oikos* appears frequently, including in the story of Cornelius (Acts 10) and the jailer in Philippi (Acts 16). This Greek word is usually translated as "household." Often, entire households would decide to follow Christ—wives, children, servants, and their families. Pastor Tom Mercer of High Point Church, a congregation of eleven thousand in southern California, sees a pattern that is still applicable in the twenty-first century. He explains:

> *Oikos*, the Greek word for "extended family," encompasses our relational worlds—anywhere from eight to fifteen people, on the average, whom God has supernaturally and strategically placed in our spheres of

influence . . . our relational worlds. We are all Christ's partners in world-change.[1]

The first step in impacting our *oikos* is writing down their names. Who are your family members? Your close friends? Coworkers? Others with whom you have regular contact? Make a commitment to pray for one each day. Ask God to use your relationship with them as a bridge they can walk across to join the community of faith.

Bethany First Church of the Nazarene in Bethany, Oklahoma, is an example of how churches grow using the *oikos* principle. The church has a close-knit feel even though more than two thousand attend on any given Sunday. There are many family connections in the church since generations of families have intermarried. Christian faith has been shared historically through the family networks in the church. This in part explains the healthy numerical growth experienced over decades.

Communities Transformed

YET *OIKOS* IS BROADER than family networks. Mercer speaks of "spheres of influence." It is through our relational worlds that transformation can spill over from families to touch entire communities. The growth of the church in sub-Saharan Africa has been astounding in part because of the *oikos* principle. Teams that project *The Jesus Film* always seek the permission of the village chief and elders before planning a showing. What is the *oikos* for a village chief and elders? The whole village! If even some leaders of the village make a clear decision to follow Christ, often many will follow Christ because of their lead.

As in Africa, so in Ephesus. The early part of Acts 19 shows the impact made not only through miracles that Paul performed but also the decisions by sorcerers to abandon their occult craft and follow Christ. The church was growing strong among both Jews and Greeks to the point that the even the religious culture

1. Mercer, "How the Oikos Grew."

of the city was being transformed. Ephesus was renowned for its temple to Artemis, the Greek goddess of the hunt, wild animals, fertility, and childbirth. Worshipers came to the temple and would purchase silver statues of Artemis. It was a lucrative trade (Acts 19:25), but Paul's message of Christ was siphoning off business as people abandoned idol worship in favor of Christianity. Disturbed by his falling revenues, a silversmith named Demetrius riled up a theater crowd, shouting: "Great is Artemis of the Ephesians!" A riot ensued. They seized a couple of traveling companions of Paul and likely would have done them bodily harm except for the intervention of the city clerk. He calmed the crowd and convinced them to use the courts and magistrates if they had a grievance (19:38).

An Anglican bishop is reported to have lamented: "Wherever the Apostle Paul went, there were riots. Wherever I go, they serve me tea and crumpets." How often do our churches resemble the bishop's lament? Yet as followers of Christ intentionally pray for their Jerusalem, their *oikos*, and model another, better way of living, God can use them to transform both their families and communities.

Summing It All Up

How can God use us to help transform our Jerusalem? To answer that question requires another: Who is our *oikos*? God has given each of us families, friends, and coworkers. This is our sphere of influence. Our mission is them! As families are changed by the love of God, so communities will be transformed for the better. Are we ready to make a difference, together?

Impacting our community will happen in many ways. One of them includes how we treat the environment. It is this topic that we'll consider in the next chapter.

Questions for Discussion

1. Susan's decision to follow Jesus impacted her sister, Lisa, who also decided to follow Christ. Share with the group another example that you know where a family relation was the means God used to draw someone to faith.

2. The term *oikos* refers to our sphere of influence. In your experience, should relationships that develop over social media be considered part of our *oikos* in the same way that face-to-face relationships are? How are these the same or different?

3. The Anglican bishop lamented his own minimal social impact as compared to that of the Apostle Paul. Think about the church where you belong. Does your church have a measurable impact on your community? If so, would most outsiders consider it negative or positive? Explain.

14

Ecology for Christ Followers

AFTER A TWENTY-MINUTE BOAT ride across choppy waves, then a thirty-minute hike in sweltering heat, I arrived with my family in a small island village off the West African coast. The pastor took us to the tent where the fledgling congregation met. For two hours, we clapped and danced to songs like "La lumière est là" (the light is here), calling people to step out of darkness into the light of Christ. The sermon was on target and the worshipers welcoming. God met with us.

Following the service, I asked the pastor about a large, dried up tree that lay on the ground adjacent to the church. He told me that they had cut it down because it was where the village priestess used to make her sacrifices to the spirits. Because of this association in the minds of the villagers, it was important—said the pastor—that they cut down the tree so that people would see that Christians had no fear of other gods. As we left that day, I wondered whether that was the only message the villagers would receive by that act. *Would they not come to view the Christians as the people who cut down trees?* How might things have been different if instead of cutting down the tree they had held a public service of dedication inviting the community leaders, consecrating the tree to the glory of God? If in Isaiah's vision "the trees of the field will clap their hands" (Isa 55:12) in praise to the LORD, then could not a tree that had been used for Satan's dark purposes be repurposed, joining instead in singing God's praise, giving shade to those who spread God's light?

God's Love for All Creation with Humanity as Caretakers

John 3:16 says that God loved the world. As we saw in an earlier chapter, the Greek word for "world" is *cosmos*. It can also be translated as "universe." In other words, God loves all that God has made. Jesus could have said: "For God so loved the *people* in the world, that he gave his only son." Yet Jesus made it far broader than that. God loved the *world*. This is consistent with the vision of the psalmist: "The LORD is good to everyone. He showers compassion on all his creation" (Ps 145:9). Psalm 104 celebrates birds, beasts of the field, and trees. Because God cares about them, he gives them life, watering and feeding them. Furthermore, our creator God did not just create at some moment in the past then stop creating. With tender love and care, God continues to create both human beings and the ecosystem that sustains us. God revels in the majestic flight of a black eagle and the intelligence of a dolphin, the comical antics of a chimp and the prowess of a cheetah. He cares about creation so much that he put human beings in charge of it with a command to rule over it wisely (Gen 1:28). God has entrusted creation to us as its stewards (Gen 2:15). We are not the owners of the earth but its caretakers. The psalmist reminds us: "The earth is the LORD's and everything in it, the world and all who live in it" (Ps 24:1). If we love God, then how can we abuse what God loves? Instead, ours is to cooperate in the renewal of creation, to be part of making everything new (Rev 21:5).

What we see in the Father we also find in the Son. Looking for a way to explain his disciples' relationship with him, Jesus chose gardening: "I am the vine, you are the branches" (John 15:15). To explain the kingdom of God, he chose the mustard seed, which grows into a tree that shelters the birds (Matt 13:31–32). Nature informs many of Jesus' parables, where Jesus draws lessons from seed, wheat, and weeds. Our Lord was at home in the outdoors and lived close to the land, riding in a boat on the Sea of Galilee, walking the open roads of Judea, praying among the olive trees at Gethsemane. What made his cursing of the fig tree (Matt 21:18–22) so memorable for the disciples was how exceptional it was for their Lord, a master who was more apt to speak of God's care for the sparrow and the lilies in the field. The picture of Jesus that emerges in the gospels is one who relishes creation, seeing in it a reflection of his Father.

Salvation as the Healing of Creation

While caring for creation is our duty as God's stewards, this is only part of the story. God intends not only to conserve creation but to heal it. Indeed, creation is part of the Bible's salvation story.

Howard Snyder notes with disappointment: "Evangelicals simply do not believe that the Bible teaches creation care as an essential part of the good news. Most Evangelical Christians do not accept environmental concern as an indispensable part of faithful Christian witness."[1] This has not always been the case. John Wesley (1703–91), particularly toward the end of his life, began to see God's salvation concern as not limited to human beings but as far broader. Snyder concludes: "John Wesley's optimism about what God could do in human experience through Jesus Christ by the Spirit tended to carry over into a measured optimism about the reform and eventual transformation of society, and ultimately of the whole creation."[2]

If creation must be *transformed*, it's because it has first been *deformed*. In Romans 8:20–22, Paul pictures creation as frustrated and groaning. It is in bondage to decay, yet optimistically waits for its liberation. Revelation 21:1 speaks of a "new heaven and a new earth." John's vision of the "first earth" is that it had passed away. Rather than seeing this as an image of unavoidable destruction, the new earth should be understood as the *renewed* earth.[3] It is the creation that has been transformed, the decay reversed, the bondage broken. It is to this task of renewal that God calls the church as

---

1. Snyder, *Creation Healed*, 46.
2. Ibid., 39.
3. Rotz, *Revelation*, 292.

part of her mission, another expression of the church "breathing out," moved by the Holy Spirit into a life-changing encounter with the world.

Earth in the Balance

Merriam-Webster's Online Dictionary defines "ecology" as a science that deals with the "relationships between groups of living things and their environments." Jonathan Twining teaches marine biology and environmental science at Eastern Nazarene College outside Boston. He grew up in the church, the son of a pastor, and loves both Christ and creation. Yet he has been saddened to see that some decide not to follow Christ because of the negative attitude many Christians have toward the environment. Twining concludes: "If Christians treat the environment like trash, those who care about the environment lose respect for what Christians have to say." In our time, applied ecology has become a prerequisite if the church wants to impact society with the message of Christ.

Professor Twining regrets that the topic of climate change has become politicized. Yet solid evidence exists that the earth is warming and it is due to human activity. Twining observes:

> Humans are pouring greenhouse gases into the atmosphere, including methane, nitrous oxide, carbon dioxide, water vapor, and chloroflourocarbons (CFCs). We put thirty billion tons of CO^2 alone into the atmosphere every year. The kind of carbon that we find in the atmosphere is directly related to the burning of fossil fuels.[4]

The long-term effects of the warming of the earth are dramatic. The melting of the ice caps in Greenland and Antarctica means that frozen water that had been on land is now running off, adding to the volume of the oceans. For this reason, ocean levels are rising, in turn threatening coastal cities around the globe, from Miami, Florida, to Maputo, Mozambique.

---

4. From an interview with the author, April 21, 2016.

Part Two: Breathing Out

In parts of the world where daily existence is a struggle, ecology may seem like a low priority. Species may go extinct, but how does that affect us? As more people live in cities, away from the land, it is more difficult for us to see the interconnectedness of all life. When asked why we should care about an obscure tree frog or butterfly, Twining replied: "What if there's a species that *we* need that depends on that tree frog or butterfly? When we lose even one species, an ecosystem can collapse." *To take care of nature is to take care of ourselves.*

Ecological challenges go beyond the question of climate change and its causes. Deforestation is also a huge challenge around the globe, but particularly in Africa. Professor Wangari Maathai, a Roman Catholic believer, won the 2004 Nobel Peace Prize for her work with the Green Belt Movement in Kenya. She grew up near Mt. Kenya and reveled as a child in the lush forests and pure streams, yet as time passed she saw negative changes as people began to consider nature merely as a commodity to exploit rather than a heritage to protect. As forests were cut or replaced with nonnative tree species, streams became murky, silted with eroding soil. The water cycle was interrupted as trees disappeared. Weather patterns changed, drying up streams and rivers and compromising catchments. Despite political opposition, she rallied women around the country, establishing tree nurseries in poor rural communities. Over time, the Green Belt Movement has planted millions of trees and raised the consciousness of the people, helping them to understand that when *we take care of nature, we take care of ourselves.* Comparing advocacy for the environment to Peter's command to the lame man at the temple gate to rise up and walk (Acts 3:1–8), at the end of her autobiography, Maathai concludes:

> As women and men continue this work of clothing this naked Earth, we are in the company of many others throughout the world who care deeply for this blue planet. We have nowhere else to go. Those of us who witness the degraded state of the environment and the suffering that comes with it cannot afford to be complacent. We continue to be restless. If we really carry the burden, we

are driven to action. We cannot tire or give up. We owe it to the present and future generations of all species to rise up and walk![5]

Fighting deforestation requires weighing long-term vs. short-term benefits. Professor Twining observes: "If you cut down a tree, you might get $500.00 for lumber, but that tree can provide you with $12,000.00 of services in a lifetime—removing air pollution, CO^2, and preventing soil erosion." While such long-term thinking is necessary, it's a hard sell for those living from hand to mouth. In rural areas throughout Africa where cooking is done with cheap charcoal made from cutting down trees, alternative ways of cooking—such as solar grills—may provide more eco-friendly solutions.

What Can the Church Do?

There are many ways that churches can model what it means to care for God's creation. In *It's Easy Being Green*, Emma Sleeth gives fifteen tips for how churches can make their buildings more eco-friendly, from starting a church garden where pesticide-free vegetables can be grown and given to the needy to an exchange program, trading possessions instead of buying new ones (and thereby saving the energy needed to produce them).[6]

In rural Africa, often the church constructs cement block buildings on land donated by the chief and village elders. While it's admirable that little wood is used in the construction, how often is the first step felling trees and clearing brush to make room for the building? Churches need to figure into the project costs for the planting and care of tree seedlings around the church once the construction is done. This will tell the community that believers care not only about the salvation of people but also the trees that give people shade in the heat and produce the oxygen that they breathe.

---

5. Maathai, *Unbowed*, 295.
6. Sleeth, *It's Easy Being Green*, ch. 9.

Part Two: Breathing Out

The same procedure applies to cities and suburbs. Paving over land with asphalt may be necessary to expand a church parking lot in Chicago or Toronto. When trees are removed, are more trees planted later around the periphery or other locations on the property to compensate for the loss of vegetation?

Summing It All Up

The old hymn reminds us: "This is my Father's world." We are not the owners of planet earth, only God's stewards to care for her. As such, God will hold us responsible for how we steward the creation. Yet God's intentions go beyond conservation to renewal, to the healing of creation. Those who do not yet follow Christ are watching us. What do they see?

As the church, we not only "breathe out" by taking care of the creation. Another aspect of our service to the world is crossing cultural barriers with the good news of the gospel. It is to this subject that we now turn.

Questions for Discussion

1. In what way should God's love for all creation—including humans, creatures, and vegetation—affect how believers live their daily lives?

2. Professor Twining claims that some have told him they aren't interested in following Christ because of how Christians mistreat the environment. Have you had similar conversations? If so, share them with the group.

3. In the case of African villagers who buy cheap charcoal to cook, we see how the destruction of the environment can be fueled by economic factors. Does one have to be rich to be "green"? Why or why not?

4. Some object that encouraging the church to get involved in ecological issues is a distraction from preaching the gospel.

How might Howard Snyder's teaching that "salvation means creation healed" help formulate a response to this objection?

15

Love without Limits: Sharing Christ Cross-Culturally

IF TRANSFORMATION IS A key biblical concept, then grace is what makes it happen. Grace—a metaphor for the transforming work of the Holy Spirit—is one of the most powerful forces known to humanity. When God's grace changes a person, it spills over to touch members of the entire family, even whole communities. Yet the book of Acts doesn't stop there. The power of the Holy Spirit, like sound waves from a sonic boom, travels outward, transforming everything in its path. The day of Pentecost in Acts 2 is the divine sonic boom, and the rest of Acts records the echoes.

No one culture or nation can trap God in a bottle, cork it, and taunt: "We have God in a bottle and we're not sharing!" The good news of Jesus Christ is good news *for all*, or it is not good news *at all*. Divine love without limits sends us out into a world that needs Christ, the church's "breathing out" in response to the energizing power of the Holy Spirit.

Into the Nations: From Centripetal to Centrifugal

In Matthew 28, our risen Lord appeared to his disciples on a hill outside Jerusalem. These were his parting words before he returned to his Father. What would he say to the men with whom he had spent three amazing years? Verses 18–20 capture the moment:

> All authority in heaven and on earth has been given to me. Therefore go and make disciples of all nations,

baptizing them in the name of the Father and of the Son and of the Holy Spirit, and teaching them to obey everything I have commanded you. And surely I am with you always, to the very end of the age.

This is the moment when disciples (followers) became sent ones (apostles). In physics, a centripetal force draws an object and keeps it in a fixed orbit, preventing it from flying outward. In the Old Testament, the people of God were to be centripetal. This is Isaiah's vision: "In the last days the mountain of the Lord's temple will be established as the highest of the mountains; it will be exalted above the hills, and all nations will stream to it" (Isa 2:2).

But something radical transpires in Matthew 28. Standing outside of Jerusalem—the very city alluded to in Isaiah's vision—Jesus does not call the disciples to a centripetal mission. Instead, their mission is to be centrifugal. Think of the mud that cakes on a tire. The faster the tire spins, the more mud that flies off in all directions. Now, God doesn't call us to fly off and make the world dirty! But the point remains: Jesus calls us not to stay but to *go and transform*. In the New Testament, the people of God are centrifugal; in the new order, God sends us on a cross-cultural mission.

Timothy Tennent describes the church's task and the centrifugal force that enables it: "The central way the Holy Spirit brings the New Creation into the present is through empowering the church to proclaim the gospel in word and deed in the midst of all contextual challenges that the present evil order presents."[1]

Getting Out of Our Comfort Zone

Those whom the church sends on a cross-cultural mission to other peoples are known as missionaries. Though the word "missionary" never appears as such in the New Testament, the Greek noun *apostolos* captures its meaning. An apostle is one who is sent with a message. In Acts 13:2–3 we read about the first missionary sending service: "While they were worshiping the Lord and fasting, the

---

1. Tennent, *Invitation to World Missions*, 96.

Part Two: Breathing Out

Holy Spirit said, 'Set apart for me Barnabas and Saul for the work to which I have called them.' So after they had fasted and prayed, they placed their hands on them and sent them off."

For centuries, many believed that the command from Christ in Matthew 28:18–20 (sometimes called the Great Commission) was only intended for the early church. William Carey (1761–1834) is known as the father of modern missions because he challenged that idea, insisting that every generation has the responsibility to obey the "go" command from Christ. Carey is said to have pleaded with fellow pastors in England about the necessity of going to other parts of the world to evangelize those who knew nothing of Christ, people who—insensitively by modern standards—were labeled "heathen." A senior minister interrupted him and railed: "Young man, sit down. When God pleases to convert the heathen world, He will do it without your help or mine."

Whether we justify our inactivity with a deterministic theology like that of Carey's skeptical colleague or some other way, let's face it: Missions pushes us out of our comfort zone. For Carey, God sent him to India where he had to learn a new language and where he and his wife faced many hardships, including the death of their five-year-old son, Peter. Yet that kind of sacrifice can be repeated today. In Cotonou, Benin (West Africa), my wife, sons, and I were part of a tight-knit group of missionary families who met every Sunday night for Bible study and prayer. It rocked our world when James—just eight years old and the son of another missionary family—succumbed to malaria. His parents and brothers went home to mourn, taking his body for a funeral and burial. Many would have understood if they had stayed home, but a year later, they returned to their Bible translation work in Benin. From their perspective, the choice was clear: People in darkness needed the light of God's Word in their own language.

What is at stake?

Missions is multifaceted. Some relocate to foreign nations to serve as nurses or doctors. Others organize remote villagers without clean water to help them dig a well. A few pilot planes, ferrying workers and supplies into remote areas. Still others put computer tech skills to work, helping keep essential tools for ministry humming. Many missionaries serve as preachers and teachers of Bible and theology, equipping believers responding to God's call to ministry as pastors, evangelists, or chaplains who will impact the world's great cities. While in the past most missionaries came from North America or Europe, now as the church matures, missionaries originate from countries around the world. Missions is "from everywhere, to everywhere."

Whatever the assignment, the motivation behind service is the same: "I'm not a missionary because I can; I'm a missionary because I must." A sense that God has spoken and said "go" will keep a missionary at his or her post when the going inevitably gets tough. Equally importantly, missionaries believe that something crucial is at stake, and that "something" is someones, human beings for whom Christ died and rose again. Knowing their suffering—both physical and spiritual—and the transforming work of New Creation that God longs to operate in their lives keeps missionaries motivated. Likewise, to care for creation and work for the preservation of the earth is to care for the people whose welfare is wrapped up with the planet that is our home.

Because missionaries love people, they also are willing to spend long hours to learn new languages. Communication in a people's heart language is essential in order to winsomely invite others to be reconciled to God through Christ. Missionaries point forward to resurrection, to a time when God will make all things new, establishing a new heaven and a new earth where God's own will live together in harmony and forever worship the Three-in-One God. What a promise, and what an incentive to surmount linguistic and cultural barriers with the good news of Jesus!

Together on the Rescue Mission

A little girl fell down inside a dark well. The village rallied together to rescue her. The well was narrow and only one man was skinny enough to fit inside the narrow shaft. Others formed a human anchor line while another found a rope. "I need your help," the man pleaded as he tied the rope around his waist. "I'm going into the well now, but I need all of you not just to lower me down but to *keep holding the rope.*"

God's great rescue mission is a team effort. There's a job for everyone to do. While many can participate in life-changing short-term mission trips of 1–2 weeks, not all can be sent long-term; vocational missions is for those well both in mind and body. Yet there are many things believers who stay home can do. Faithful prayers offered for lonely missionaries deployed far from home make a difference, and an encouraging note by e-mail or social media saying "I prayed for you today" often comes at a missionary's lowest moment. If God has blessed you with resources beyond your daily needs, make a monthly pledge to help pay a missionary's salary. Even those with modest income may be surprised how much can be given if one gives up a designer cup of coffee or sugar-laden soft drinks. Your health will benefit and so will the cause of global missions.

Summing It All Up

Jesus commands us to go into all the world to make disciples. God the Holy Spirit empowers the church as she "breathes out," sending her across language and cultural barriers with the message of the gospel. The new creation message is that God wants to renew all things, the earth and all who inhabit it. Transformation happens when people are reconciled to God through Christ, yet this rescue mission will only succeed if the whole church works together. Each of us has a part to play. What will *your* contribution be?

Questions for Discussion

1. Think about your church in relation to your community. Would you describe your efforts as centripetal or centrifugal? Is it possible (even desirable) to have both?

2. The author describes missionary work as crossing cultural and linguistic barriers. Is it always necessary to travel to another country to do such work? What missionary opportunities can be found close to home?

3. William Carey and his wife lost a son while in India. Think about your own life and availability to God. What would you consider too great a price to pay in order that someone else might learn about Christ and follow him?

4. We often don't think about creation care as part of missionary work. Do you agree with the author's suggestion that taking care of the environment is another way of caring for people? Why or why not?

5. In what ways has your church been part of "holding the rope" for missionaries? Has anyone from your community of faith undertaken missionary work long-term? How can we create an atmosphere in the church where both youth and adults are open to God's call to cross-cultural service?

Conclusion

MERE ECCLESIOLOGY: FINDING YOUR Place in the Church's Mission underscores what no church can do without and long survive. This essential function is spiritual respiration, "breathing in" God's life-giving Spirit and "breathing out" in transformational service to the world.

Breathing in encompasses many practices that move us closer to God and bind us together as a team. When we worship together, the wind of the Holy Spirit blows through the church, even as the Spirit did on the Day of Pentecost, transforming, cleansing, and empowering God's people. Through preaching, the Eucharist, and baptism, we grow deeper in our faith, enticing others to join us on the journey. Through Christian education and small groups, we acknowledge that growth happens best when it happens in community. God calls his people to pray and to fast, drawing nearer to the One who longs to draw near to us.

Yet breathing in—as important as it is—remains incomplete. Energized by the Holy Spirit, the church breaths out, moving into the world in ways that cannot help but make a positive change. God longs to transform all of creation. To do so, he sends the church and its disciples on a mission of healing and deliverance. With gifts and graces given by the Holy Spirit, each of us discovers our calling, the unique contribution that God wants us to make in the world. Love pushes us to impact communities nearby and far away, driving us to surmount all cultural barriers, taking the good news of Jesus Christ to a world that too often is hopeless. And as we love people, we work to restore the earth, the place where all

Conclusion

live and where God is establishing his kingdom. The task is enormous, yet the Spirit who impels us is sufficient for every challenge.

It's time for the church to stop holding her breath. *What is your place in the church's mission?* Pray for God to direct you to the niche that you are uniquely qualified to fill. Let us breathe in and let us breathe out. The God who transforms us also sends us out—in the power of the Holy Spirit—to transform the world. What a mission!

Bibliography

Crofford, Gregory, and Maluleka, Mashangu. "Let Them Call for the Elders of the Church: Divine Healing and the Church of the Nazarene in South Africa." *Didache: Faithful Teaching* 13 (2014) n.p. http://didache.nazarene.org/index.php/gtc2013/context/987-healing-crofiord-maluleka-eng-1/file.

Earle, Ralph. *Word Meanings in the New Testament*. Kansas City: Beacon Hill, 1986.

Evans, Robert. "6 Tricks I Learned as a Faith Healer (for Scamming You)." *Cracked.com*, September 1, 2014. http://www.cracked.com/personal-experiences-1454-6-tricks-i-learned-as-faith-healer-for-scamming-you.html.

"Homily." *New Advent Catholic Encyclopedia*. http://www.newadvent.org/cathen/07448a.htm.

Lewis, C. S. *Mere Christianity*. 1943. Reprint, New York: Macmillan, 1979.

———. *The Screwtape Letters*. 1941. Reprint, HarperCollins e-book, 2009.

Maathai, Wangari. *Unbowed: A Memoir*. New York: Knopf, 2006.

Mahomoodally, M. Fazwi. "Traditional Medicines in Africa: An Appraisal of Ten Potent African Medicinal Plants." *Evidence-Based Complementary and Alternative Medicine* 2013 (2103) 14 pp. http://www.hindawi.com/journals/ecam/2013/617459.

Mahoney, Kelli. "Biblical Verses on Fasting." *Christian Teens* (website). http://christianteens.about.com/od/christianliving/a/VersesOnFasting.htm.

Mercer, Tom. "How the Oikos Grew High Desert Church to 11,000 Attenders." Published March 22, 2010, SermonCentral.com. http://www.sermoncentral.com/pastors-preaching-articles/tom-mercer-how-the-oikos-grew-high-desert-church-to-11000-attenders-728.asp.

Noble, Thomas A. *Holy Trinity, Holy People: The Historic Doctrine of Christian Perfecting*. Kindle ed. Eugene, OR: Cascade, 2013.

Pinnock, Clark. *Flame of Love: A Theology of the Holy Spirit*. Downers Grove: InterVarsity, 1996.

Powell, Kara E., and Chap Clark. *Sticky Faith: Everyday Ideas to Build Lasting Faith in Your Kids*. Grand Rapids: Zondervan, 2011.

Bibliography

Rotz, Carol. *Revelation*. New Beacon Bible Commentary. Kansas City: Beacon Hill, 2012.

Simpson, A. B. *The Gospel of Healing*. In *Healing: The Three Great Classics on Divine Healing*. Compiled and edited by Jonathan L. Graf. Camp Hill, PA: Christian Publications, 1992.

Sleeth, Emma. *It's Easy Being Green*. Grand Rapids: Zondervan, 2008.

Snyder, Howard A. *Salvation Means Creation Healed: The Ecology of Sin and Grace; Overcoming the Divorce between Heaven and Earth*. With Joel Scandrett. Eugene, OR: Cascade, 2011.

Stott, John R. W. *Between Two Worlds: The Art of Preaching in the Twentieth Century*. Grand Rapids: Eerdmans, 2000.

Tennent, Timothy C. *An Invitation to World Missions: A Trinitarian Missiology for the 21st Century*. Grand Rapids: Kregel, 2010.

Zirulnick, Ariel. "Kenya 'Miracle Worker' Scandal Hits Deep Faith in Churches." *Christian Science Monitor*, November 20, 2014. http://www.csmonitor.com/World/Africa/2014/1120/Kenya-miracle-healer-scandal-hits-deep-faith-in-churches.

Zweigle, Grant. *Worship, Wonder, and Way: Reimagining Evangelism as Missional Practice*. Kansas City: Beacon Hill, 2015.

www.ingramcontent.com/pod-product-compliance
Lightning Source LLC
Chambersburg PA
CBHW070930160426
43193CB00011B/1633